MW00411799

NO MATTER WHAT!

My Journey to the
Hem of His Garment

Aunt Jan,
Bonnie wanted you to
take this journey with me!
Love,
Marcia Marron

By

Marcia Buterakos Marron

Copyright © 2019 Marcia Buterakos Marron

All rights reserved. No part of this book may be reproduced or transmitted in any form or by any means, electronically or mechanically, including photocopying, recording, or by an information storage and retrieval system without permission in writing from the author of this book.

ISBN: 9781797468242

Published by:
Marcia Buterakos Marron

Edited by:
Dr. Ruth L. Baskerville
www.ruthbaskerville.com

Cover Design by:
Rob Williams, Designer
ilovemycover.com

Dedication

I dedicate this book to my father, Michael Buterakos, my mother, Marcella Buterakos, and my sister, Maria Buterakos.

My Greek Dad, loving, strong, mighty, loyal, and courageous. I was his princess. He made me believe I could do anything because he believed in me.

My all-American Mom, fearless, kind, adoring, organized and a force to be reckoned with. She was my daily cheerleader, always encouraging me and supporting my every dream.

My sister, a spit-fire! She was beautiful, challenging, pesty, loving and a friend to all. She emulated me, as her older sister, but she had an independence that rivaled mine.

Marcia Buterakos Marron

Acknowledgements

I could not have written this book without the love and moral support and encouragement of my children, Michael, Kyle, Makayla and my daughter in love Claudia. My love for them is what got me through the toughest of times. They never left my side, and I consider them to be my heart beat.

Throughout my entire life, I had the guidance of my Auntie Kaye, my mother's sister. She is my confidant, my friend and my second mother. She is a wise woman who knew how and when to bring scriptures to me that would change my life.

Finally, I humbly acknowledge my husband, Kevin Marron, who is my covenant life partner. He has been God's instrument in prodding me to write this book. He's my best friend, always ready with the right word or touch to calm my spirit at the end of every day. I cherish him dearly. Without his inspiration and motivation, I could never have accomplished this task.

Marcia Buterakos Marron

Introduction

"Now a woman, having a flow of blood for twelve years, who had spent all her livelihood on physicians and could not be healed by any, [44] came from behind and touched the border of His garment. And immediately her flow of blood stopped. [45] And Jesus said, "Who touched Me?"

When all denied it, Peter and those with him said, "Master, the multitudes throng and press You and You say, 'Who touched Me?'"

[46] But Jesus said, "Somebody touched Me, for I perceived power going out from Me." [47] Now when the woman saw that she was not hidden, she came trembling; and falling down before Him, she declared to Him in the presence of all the people the reason she had touched Him and how she was healed immediately" (Luke 8:43-47 NKJV).

This book is my story — all of it! I lived every day of it, and God placed upon my heart the need to share it. So much in the *Bible* resonates with me, but the story of the woman with the issue of blood is particularly meaningful because she reached a level of desperation in her life where nothing mattered more than touching the hem of Jesus' garment.

For me, it was reaching a point where nothing else mattered but being forgiven, healed and set free by my Lord, Jesus Christ.

Marcia Buterakos Marron

Table of Contents

Chapter 1
In The Beginning, God Created Greeks!

If I had to think of one word to summarize my earliest childhood memories, it would be *"Happy."* I knew from the moment I could talk that my parents loved me more than the air they breathed. God poured out an extra special amount of affection upon His "Greek people," causing them to be almost covetous with their adoration for their children. My surroundings were not elaborate, but my food was always plentiful and made just the way my little taste buds liked it. My covers were soft and big enough to wrap me in my bed like I was snuggled in a cocoon of safety. Dad and Mom showered me with kisses, just because I woke up and walked into the kitchen with my little brown teddy bear tucked under my arm and asked for milk.

When I was about three or four years old, I began having bad dreams that woke me in the night. I saw my house burning and everyone running outside. When I followed, both of my parents were gone from my sight and I was alone. In my haste to run as fast as my parents, I forgot to grab my teddy bear, so I stood outside my burning home, shivering and crying and not knowing which way to go to find my security again.

When I awoke each time, with little variation in the contents of the dreams, I knew that something was always separating me from my parents and leaving me alone and unprotected, without direction. Then, I climbed out of my bed, grabbed my teddy bear, and ran to my parents' bedroom, where they always awoke and scooped me up and placed me in their warm bed, right between them. Instantly, I fell back asleep and dreamed the dreams of happy little girls until we all woke together the next morning. No matter how many times I had bad dreams, and no matter how many years during my early childhood that I had the bad dreams, my parents always reinstated my sense of security and showed me their unconditional love until I fell peacefully back to sleep in their loving arms.

Don't get me wrong about my blissful childhood. Dad's first name was Michael, probably because the most powerful Angel in the *Holy Bible* was "Michael." He was a full-blooded Greek Orthodox man who stood a little less than six feet tall and weighed under two hundred pounds. He was handsome and had a silvery tone to his voice. But when he came into the house, it was like "the Captain is on the bridge!" Even Mom straightened her posture initially, although she definitely could hold her own. Dad was born in the USA, but came from Greek immigrants who settled in Michigan with the expectation that the children would be raised in the Greek faith. That was not just his expectation, but every other living family member, all of whom were Greek! If you saw the movie, *My Big Fat Greek Wedding,* I could relate to every scene.

That brings me to describing my mother, whose real name was Marcella. In the movie, there's a memorable line about the father making all the decisions, but the mother is the "neck." Everyone knows the neck turns the head and the body follows. Well my Mom was definitely the "neck." She described herself as a *"Heinz57"* mother – a bit southern and a bit northern. She was born in the "show me" state; Missouri and was a Baptist. Oh, she and Dad fell in love easy enough, but when she met his family, they were completely against the marriage because she was not

Greek. Their disdain turned to joy, however, when Mom promised she would raise her children in the Greek Orthodox Church. Mom was wise not to go up against a tidal wave of opposition throughout her marriage. Mom was strong and took no grief from anyone. On several occasions, such as birthdays or Christmas, if a gift she gave was the wrong size or color, we would just pretend it was right because no one wanted to go with her to make the exchange!

My mother – Marcella -- was known to put forth her best argument if she could not find the gift in the right size or color! Soon everyone standing around the counter would know of her displeasure when she was told, *"We do not give cash refunds!"* I would find myself making any excuse to wait for her outside the store. While this sounds harsh there was also something of a comfort knowing that in this outward strength there was a kinder, gentler woman who was the best at mending scrapes or bruises, and offering a hug and kiss to any pain I was feeling. She was, along with my Dad, my greatest cheerleader.

They both made me feel like there was nothing I could not achieve. From ballet as a young child, to running for Student Council President in the 8th grade, to taking part in every musical in high school, there they were, cheering me on. My gift back to them was good grades, always trying hard to make them feel proud, and giving them my love and admiration in my final speech at my high school graduation. From a little girl to taking me to visit colleges then on to plan my very own Big Fat Greek Wedding, I knew my parents always had me close and I never ever doubted their love for me. While Mom could "cuss like a sailor," her favorite place was at home taking care of her family. She was well kept, her home was always immaculate and many times she would shoo us out of her kitchen, stating, *"You girls just do not know how to load the dishwasher, or stir the gravy on the stove."* She left us to setting the table and looking and acting like well behaved young ladies.

Six years after me came my little sister, Maria, and I had to share my parents with this stranger. While I was focused on turning ten and living the life of a double-digit kid, my little sister wanted to follow me and copy everything I did. I remember thinking she is a real pain. But my parents loved her with the same intensity as they loved me, and eventually, I decided to let her live and not just kill her off so I could be an only child again.

I truly wanted and adored my little sister. However, when my closest Aunt, who would always stop by to see *me*, began to come even more often, and stated she had come to see the "baby," I had no problem blurting out, "Well if you have only come to see her, just go home!" She would laugh out loud upon hearing that remark, and would always hug me and tell me how very much she loved me! I quickly loved the "4 Ms" – Michael, Marcella, Marcia and Maria. We were the "fabulous four," and our family unit was singular.

However, as soon as my little sister was no longer a baby, she became a pest to me. She was always following me around, always wanting to play with my friends and me. I made every excuse to exclude her from all of that. After all, she was six years younger than I, and that was all the excuse I needed. Much to my chagrin, my mother would always find a way to include her in everything! She and I were both green-eyed and had blonde hair. We got none of the Greek traits that most of my cousins had -- brown eyes, olive skin, and dark shiny hair. However, I would soon discover that the more sun I got as a teenager, the more my skin resembled my Greek side. I loved that because I believe I was the only Greek girl in all the schools I attended!

11

Religion was also a big part of "growing up Greek." I went to Greek School, had a phonics hymnal that allowed me to sing in the choir, and attended services regularly at our local Greek Orthodox Church where I had my early teachings of faith, and learned the importance of our rich traditions. Easter was my favorite holiday, not because Jesus rose from the dead, but because I loved the sweet *"Koulourakia"* cookies my mother always made, and the red hardboiled eggs given out at church. Oh, yes, the teaching of why Jesus Christ is at the center of our lives didn't escape me either, but growing up, I sought the pleasures of the flesh before those of the spirit! I have such wonderful memories beyond church, such as attending Greek dances and Greek Festivals. It's well known that food and laughter are a big part of the everyday lives of the big Greek extended and close-knit family. I felt immensely secure knowing I belonged right here.

I didn't date much in high school because my Dad had a strict rule that if any boy wanted to take me out, he had to come and meet my family, and then Dad would take a week to decide if I could go. So I had exactly one boy in high school willing to go through the scrutiny to abide by my father's rules. He came to my home and shook my Dad's hand firmly, as if to prove that he had the strength to take care of me for the duration of a date. He asked to take me out, and one week later, Dad gave consent. I just hoped this boy didn't forget all about me and find someone else because when you're in high school, a week is like an eternity.

We had a few dates, but since he was a year older than I, he graduated and left for college while I was finishing my junior year. We were probably too young and immature to contemplate a lasting relationship anyway, so we parted as friends. I spent my summer working at a local clothing store in the mall, trying not to imagine my life in a convent just because no other boy had the fortitude that this one had.

One day, while I was straightening up a pile of sweaters, a particularly handsome young man walked into the store and was speaking to the manager. As I glanced in his direction, our eyes met and my heart melted instantly. "Handsome man" had a toned and gorgeous physique, a beautiful, thick head of dark hair that dipped slightly over one eye, adding to his sex appeal. And he parted his lips slightly to give me a tiny smile before returning his focus to the manager.

I immediately looked away and walked away, almost losing my balance and falling to the floor because I hadn't seen the tall clothing stand that was right in front of my face. When I used the stand to steady myself, I lowered my head a little and glanced back in the direction of Handsome Man, only to find that he had left the store.

Two days later, he returned and said his name was "Josh," after which he asked if I would have a *Coke* with him when I had my next break. My heart was jumping out of my chest, as I weakly said, "Yes, sure, that would be nice." I took my next break early, and we went to the sweet shop in the mall where all the teens hung out. I enjoyed being seen with this attractive man. As we sipped our sodas, I volunteered that my Dad was an old-fashioned Greek father, overly protective of his daughters and suspicious of every male younger than an adult. I asked if we might not continue to meet at the store and share a *Coke* and a conversation. He agreed.

However, after about five or six "mini-dates," Josh said he would take his chances meeting Dad because he had strong feelings for me and wanted to show me what a real date looked like. I was too nervous to be with him when he met Dad, so I made sure I was at work when I gave him my address. I also prepared Dad to meet this young man by saying he was nineteen years old, when really he was twenty. I was a nervous wreck, thinking of a dozen unpleasant scenarios until I saw him come through the door of the clothing store with a big grin on his face. Phew! Dad had let him live!

We spent the rest of that summer golfing, swimming, boating, going to the movies, and talking endlessly via phone, since that was the only method of communication back then. Mind you, we had one phone in the house that hung from the wall in the kitchen, so not only was privacy non-existent, but also other family members bothered you constantly because they *needed* to use the phone.

My whole family liked Josh, but especially my Dad, who surprised all of us by inviting this man's whole family to dinner. He had seven brothers and two sisters so his family was considerably larger than ours, with only two girls. I was enjoying the typical Greek dinner that Mom prepared, and just as I put another bite of meat into my mouth, the unexpected happened. Dad went around the table asking each of Josh's siblings their ages. When he got to him, it was painfully obvious that either he was older than nineteen or he was a twin that neither of his parents acknowledged. Dad was quick, doing the math in his head with lightning speed staring hard at me.

I had no choice but to tell the truth, absolutely certain that I would never see this man again. Yep, I would live out my life as an old maid or in a convent for celibate Nuns, and my fate would be decided the moment the company left. But to my surprise, Dad flashed a big grin and said to me, *"Well played!"* The truth was Dad really liked this young man, and more importantly Josh and I were deeply in love. This was my one true love, forever and ever.

It was my senior year, and Josh was returning to college in Indiana, four hours away. He was in a five-year program as a pre-law student, and was in his third year. We corresponded regularly, and that summer, we both worked in local places in our hometown of Flint, Michigan. Dad was an established icon in the town, managing the largest and finest clothier. He was impeccably dressed and made sure his family was also. He set the fashion standard for what everyone else wore, and my sister and I felt special and important because of it.

At the end of that summer, I was going to college in Indiana, but not near his university. I chose my institution of higher learning because it was a Lutheran College my Dad wanted me to attend. Josh would be completing his fourth year, only lacking a semester of school that he could take next year. Like the previous year, we corresponded all the time, wishing we could be together, but being patient for the day that would materialize.

That Thanksgiving, he stepped right up to Dad and asked for my hand in marriage. He hadn't even asked me first, but I didn't care. Dad said, *"Yes,"* and so did I. Once I was engaged to be married, my relationship with my sister changed. She would be my Maid of Honor and we became quite close. She was twelve and I was barely out of high school when I got married. Now the fun in our sisters' relationship would begin because I was no longer a teen being annoyed by an elementary school child. She looked up to me, hoping one day she would find her one, true love, just like I did. My advice was to be patient because the right man would come at the right time. And besides, I had softened Dad up so my sister's suitors would have none of the pressure my two boyfriends had. She was lucky!

My fiancé and I returned to our respective universities, happily anticipating the day when we would be married. I had only completed one semester of college when my parents thought it best that I drop out and come home to help plan my wedding. I was obedient, of course, but I had to say I delighted in earning the *"Mrs. Degree,"* since I successfully landed a husband! Truthfully, my Mom and my aunts and grandmother fought for control of my wedding, so there was little for me to actually approve. But I understood that the real reason I was home was that Dad and Mom wanted to spend every day and night with their little girl until she married and left to spend the rest of her life with her husband.

Once I was engaged, the only thing upon which everyone agreed was that we would be married in my Greek Orthodox Church. That was non-negotiable. However, every adult female in my family gave opinions of what I should wear, who should attend, what should be served, and what the groom must commit to do in order to keep me "in the style of living to which I had been accustomed all my life." I watched my world spinning all around me, but dared not interfere with the plans of the elders. After all, I was only the bride, and therefore the last person worthy of an opinion about what my wedding day would look like.

My home was bustling with plans for flowers, caterers, decorations, and had there not been a movie made, entitled *My Big Fat Greek Wedding!"* my wedding day would have been the movie. I had ten bridesmaids and he had ten groomsmen. All of them could be at the altar, but only Greek Orthodox persons could participate in the actual ceremony on the altar. So my young sister was my Maid of Honor, and a Greek Orthodox cousin had to stand in for the official best man until our vows were exchanged.

There was loud and happy music, food and drink, laughter, and many hugs and kisses given among all the guests. Since my fiancé's family didn't speak Greek, our presiding Priest, who conducted the ceremony in Greek was assisted by another Priest who spoke the same words in English. You can imagine the length of my wedding day! It was traditional and beautiful, and I would not have had my special day done any other way. We were so happy!

My husband had one last semester before graduation, so I went with him, excited to begin my life as a wife of a pre-law student, living in modest campus housing. Because Indiana was only four hours from Michigan, our goodbyes were less tearful than they would have been otherwise. We were coming back often, and when he finished school, we were coming home for good. Surely he would find a good law school close to home, since both our families lived close to each other.

It was my Dad who encouraged me often, saying that, although he provided well for his family, I would have much more as the wife of a lawyer. My job was to be supportive, submissive, and patient, knowing that any sacrifices I made along the way would benefit me later. I believed Dad about everything, and I believed him about this, too. My life would be *special,* as the wife of a prominent attorney. I felt that "all was right with the world!"

Chapter 1 Reflections:
Ephesians 6:2-3 New King James Version (NKJV) –
"Honor your father and mother, which is the first commandment with promise: that it may be well with you and you may live long on earth."

Have you had an attitude of honor toward your earthly parents? Why or why not? Ask the Lord to reveal areas of your relationship with your parents that may need work, and write those down here.

17

Chapter 2
The Unimaginable Happens!

All *was* right with the world – until it wasn't! Josh finished college with great scores and a world of opportunities for law school awaiting him. We had survived the cramped college dorm housing, but we enjoyed his college friends and the beautiful landscape around the college in Indiana. We were anxious to return home, where our relatives and friends lived. We never discussed as a married couple where Josh would go to law school, but I just assumed that, since one of his acceptances was in Michigan, he would attend there. We could live near our parents, and I would work while he was in law school. Josh knew how close I was to my parents, and how I longed to see them during the brief time we were away during his last semester of college. Surely, he would want to make me happy if it lined up with his career goal of becoming a lawyer!

As it turned out, Josh did seriously consider Michigan, but he also considered Colorado, which was about a two-day car trip from our home. He made his decision so quickly that I had no time to insist on my input in such a big decision. I kept remembering Dad's words that I should be supportive and submissive because my future would be brighter than any family member before me. So, although my heart was aching, almost breaking, I silently accepted the fact that we were moving very far away from the home and the family I dearly loved. My parents accepted Josh's decision without protest because he was the head of our household, and especially Dad knew the importance of no family going against what the father, or in our case, the husband did.

I remember crying when I was alone packing, never letting anyone see my tears. I promised myself that life would be good in Colorado because Josh and I were in love and we had each other. I also accepted the fact that he needed to go to law school full-time, since the classes and homework would keep him in the university law library well into the night many times per week. That meant I needed a job with enough income to support both of us, but since I had settled for a "Mrs. Degree," my options were narrow.

The year was 1976, and this time our goodbyes were long and tearful. Everyone cried except for Josh and Dad. My extended family came to say goodbye too, and the scene looked like those professional mourners at Greek funerals. There was much wailing and loud crying, interspersed with hugging and kissing. But finally, we got in our car and began the very long drive to Boulder, Colorado.

Josh must have noticed how quiet I was for the first several hours of our journey, but he pretended I was fine because he needed me to be fine. How else could we make it? Among the saddest days of my life was at a rest stop at a *Pizza Hut* in Kansas. I loved pizza, but I found myself picking at my food, missing my parents and my sister. Josh leaned across the table and said, *"I'm glad we're going far from home because I was a little jealous of the closeness you had with your family – much closer than I was with mine. But I needed to know if you would really leave your Dad and come away with me, no matter the distance."* Josh gave me a half grin as he settled back in his chair to eat his pizza. But I felt like I didn't know this man whom I had married. How could he say such a thing? Was he always a manipulator of other people's feelings, or just those of his young wife? I had never seen the insecurity that I

20

now saw so plainly. I knew for a fact that my Dad loved and respected Josh, and yet he was obviously threatened by my father's strength. I felt trapped and sick, but there was no turning back. I clung to Dad's advice about life getting better for me as a lawyer's wife.

We arrived at our new "home," which was a small residence looking like a summer bungalow, except there were few windows and nearly every wall was thick concrete. We had to go to the hardware store for the special drill that was needed to put a nail into these walls, but that drill allowed us to hang a few pictures so that we felt like we had a home.

Josh was happy with his professors, his curriculum, and his colleagues, all of them studying to be lawyers. I, on the other hand, worked a low-paying job full-time in order to put my husband through law school. I understood the sacrifice I had to make, and made myself find joy in my circumstances. But in the back of my mind, I was beginning to resent Josh because Dad offered to give or lend us money before we left, but Josh was too proud to take a penny. We could have used a financial cushion, in case I ever got sick and had to miss a day of work. Josh's silly pride caused me to work when I had a headache or a cold. I didn't miss work because *we* needed the money.

During this time, I continued a long-distance, but good relationship with my parents. My parents were my greatest cheerleaders, and it seemed like every time I heard their voices, I was cheered up. The time before graduation went slowly, and the only bright spots in my life were when my parents came to visit us, and when my sister, Maria flew all by herself to be with us for a few days.

Once I had moved out of our home with my new husband, Maria and I spent long hours on the phone sharing secrets and giggling about our parents. When she asked for advice about dating and school and friends who stab you in the back, I willingly gave it. But I was careful not to infringe upon her need to grow up, just like I had done.

There was a time when I arranged for my sister to come and visit my husband and me, and I don't know if it was she or I who was most proud of her maneuvering through airports successfully. I was never happier to see anyone than that time my baby sister, Maria, came to see us. But I'm getting ahead of my story. Suffice it to say that when I was an only child, my parents and I had a three-person unbreakable bond. The *Holy Bible* speaks of the strength of a three-cord braid. When Maria arrived and I realized I couldn't send her back, I grew to love her dearly, and our four-member family was as solid as a rock. Having her right next to me for a short time was like touching my parents – maybe even touching Heaven. Our time was too short, and she returned home.

The bright spot in my life was when Josh and I found a neighborhood Baptist church with an incredibly welcoming congregation and Pastor. We both felt instinctively that this was the place where we could learn about Jesus Christ and grow in our faith. Growing up, I had a lot of "head knowledge" from going to church every Sunday with my extended family. Everyone went to church, and then everyone had Sunday dinner with one of the elder family members. We never talked about the scripture or the leader's message once we left the church. No, we talked about the food we were about to enjoy, or life for different family members. So church was something you "did" once weekly, and sometimes in the middle of the week.

At this point in my life, I, of course, knew Jesus was the Son of God, that He came to bring salvation to a corrupt world, and that only He, being without sin, could make the supreme sacrifice of dying on the cross for the sins of all mankind. Reading the *Holy Bible* was like reading any other book. *"Studying"* the *Holy Bible* in order to have a relationship with our Father in Heaven was a foreign concept to us and to all the families around us. We believed we were good Christians who would enter Heaven when we died. It was as simple as that!

This Baptist church had a place in its Sunday worship where parishioners could make a public profession of their faith, or seek prayer, or cry and pray at the altar. My heart seemed to pull me to the church as often as the doors were open, and eventually, it pulled me to the altar. I asked Jesus to come into my heart and be Lord of my life. Instantly, I felt what I later learned was the Holy Spirit come inside of me, and I had unspeakable joy. Still, I left the church wanting to be baptized because I wanted to be obedient to all of what Jesus Christ had done for me.

I believe I can honestly say I heard Him calling me forth to get baptized, which I did. It was among the most wonderful experiences of my life, and I was incredibly happy when Josh decided to get baptized with me, as a couple. I was a baby Christian. I took Jesus everywhere I went. It was a glorious transformation that started pretty soon after we moved to Boulder, Colorado. Maybe God was bringing me there, just to find Him through worship at this little Baptist church. This was a turning point in my attitude about myself. I really was a child of God and there was so much I needed to learn by reading the Word of God. I began reading, and soon realized that the same passage had different meanings. The longer I read, the more God revealed to me about the deeper meaning of each scripture. Josh was more of a "Sunday" Christian, but I was confident that if I continued to read and study, he would want to do the same.

I loved talking about God and the *Holy Bible* to my parents and my sister when we shared everything each week. My mother was delighted with my hunger for Christ; however, Dad was a bit confused, as he could not imagine attending any church other than the Greek Orthodox Church. At this time my mother and sister began going back to Mom's roots as a Baptist, and my sister, Maria, experienced the same salvation I had! I actually have a letter she sent me after she was saved. Needless to say it wasn't long before my Dad began going to church with them and had his own touch from the Lord! Wow! Who would have thought that the "4 Ms" -- Michael, Marcella, Marcia and Maria -- would all meet Jesus as their Lord and Savior! No, my dad was NOT baptized!

My parents used to call me faithfully every week, but on Sunday, June 18, 1978, they didn't call me. I wasn't upset at all because they had called on the 17th to announce they were going to my grandparents on Father's Day, the 18th. Each week when we had our phone time together, Dad would always encourage me to suppress any anxiety or depression I may have, and to keep my "eyes on the prize" of being *"Mrs. Lawyer"* sooner than I thought. I knew his pep talk by heart, and yet I still needed to hear his soothing words in order to get through another week until the next time I talked to my parents. My dad would always end our phone calls by saying, *"Hang in there,"* and I'd always respond, "You know I will, Dad."

Although I was not scheduled to speak to my parents that Sunday, I wanted to wish my Dad a Happy Father's Day. So I called my grandmother and asked to speak to Dad. She said they hadn't arrived yet, and it was well past lunchtime. I sensed some concern in her voice, but nothing to seriously worry about. But then, maybe it was the Holy Spirit speaking to me, but something told me to ask Grandma to call the Michigan

State Police. She did call, and when she called me back, she told me they were sending officers to her house to tell her what had happened. My husband told me they wouldn't send police to the house unless there had been a death. I thought that couldn't possibly be true. I think I yelled at him for the first time in our marriage, saying he needed to stop talking foolishness. My parents would have a plausible explanation for being late to lunch, once they arrived.

Josh got really quiet, not wanting to upset me. But he began to pace around the kitchen and it made me nervous. We sat there for an hour, which seemed like an eternity. During that hour, it was almost as if time stood still. I started to think which parent could have died, although I was praying hard that everyone would be OK. Finally the phone rang and startled me back to reality. Josh sprang to his feet and raced for the phone, but I was already standing by the phone at the moment, so I grabbed it and tried to suppress my frantic voice when I said, "Hello." An officer had, in fact, arrived at my grandparents' home, and he spoke instead of Grandma. He asked to talk to my husband, and I immediately felt agitated because I should be the first to learn what happened to one of my three family members – that's *if* anyone had died. My Grandma had insisted that the officer talk to Josh and not me.

Josh was now standing very close to me, and he gently took the phone from my hand and gave the officer his name. I sat at the kitchen table, almost paralyzed in an attempt to hear every word that was spoken. Josh didn't look at me at first, but stared straight at the wall on which the phone was mounted.

He crossed the kitchen slowly, involuntarily, as his face became void of color. He looked "like he had seen a ghost," and he sunk into the kitchen chair as if his body were twice as heavy as it really was. My palms were sweating and I was holding my breath, daring not to cry until I heard all the news. Both our hearts were racing, and then I saw Josh put his head in his hands, almost dropping the phone to the floor. He quickly retrieved it and returned it to his ear. He cleared his throat and asked the officer to repeat what Josh thought he had just heard.

I remember him saying, *"All three of them?"* He waited for the officer to respond before he ended the conversation with, *"Thank you for calling."* Why didn't he ask to speak to Grandma again? Why didn't he let me speak to the officer or Grandma? WHAT WAS GOING ON? As my mind became a jumble of unanswered questions, Josh stood over me and he grabbed me by my shoulders and pulled me to a standing position. My eyes were focused on his, and he put his arms completely around me and whispered, *"Your mom, your dad and your sister have been killed in a head-on collision."* I fell to the floor, saying in a broken sentence that it couldn't be true. There had been a terrible mistake – a misunderstanding. But no, my entire family had not just died on Father's Day in Flint, Michigan.

I must have passed out from shock because the next thing I remember was Josh kneeling on the floor beside me, gently patting my face, saying he was leaving me just long enough to get me a glass of water. He never took his eyes off me while he went to the sink and returned to me on the floor with a glass of water to sip. I couldn't even find my mouth, so Josh made sure some water went down my throat. He was back on the floor with me, holding me. We sat there, both of us crying and crying. We knew we had to get it together fast, but neither of us had the strength to think coherently until we could manage to stop crying.

Quite suddenly, I felt a surge of energy, as if I could stand up, so I motioned to Josh to help me up. As quickly as I began crying, I stopped, which we both knew was a dangerous sign, but neither of us addressed that fact at that moment. Josh was wiping a steady stream of tears the whole time he held me and tried to find words of comfort. He, too, must have been in shock. The whole thing was like a bad dream from which we both wanted to emerge. But it was very real, and utterly sad. The unthinkable, the unimaginable had just happened!

I would describe my behavior at that moment as being "temporarily insane." I raised my voice, shouting that we had to get home immediately. We had to go right now, and we definitely had to fly because time was of the essence. Josh had never seen me so irritated and frantic, and he tried to bring forth the practical fact that we lacked the money to fly home. We would have to drive, which would take about two days.

I refused to hear anything about our finances. I rushed upstairs to the bedroom, dragging all our suitcases from the closet at the same time. Josh followed. Sunday was the day we did laundry after church, and this particular Sunday, nearly everything we owned needed washing. I just started to put dirty clothes in the suitcase, utterly confused about the substance of what I was packing. I couldn't focus logically upon what different kinds of clothing we would need for at least the next week. There would be a viewing and a funeral, and I would need to pack one or more dresses. Nope! Random clothing items continued to fill the first two suitcases, and Josh dared not stop my packing.

In the midst of all this chaos, there was knock at the door, and the persons with whom we were scheduled to play tennis earlier that day asked if we had forgotten our date. We stood in the doorway, speechless. We couldn't even comprehend the date we forgot, or the friends we should have met that afternoon. I couldn't even speak, but Josh blurted out that my whole family just died and we needed to get to Michigan very fast. He must have added that we lacked the funds to fly, but couldn't take the time to drive. We needed help right away. Our friends gave us a few comforting words and said they would return shortly.

We didn't know it at the time, but our friends went to the church and explained the situation for us. They said we had to fly because we were both in shock, and we were in no condition to drive. On top of that, we were needed home as quickly as we could get there. Our church leaders bought us one-way tickets home, since we didn't know how long we would be gone. Our tennis friends made the flight arrangements and took us to the airport. All we had to do was pack, and the suitcases we were taking were not just full of dirty clothes, but were also void of the different sets of clothing we would need when we got to Michigan.

All the way to the airport, I cried, and then stopped crying, and then cried some more. By the time we got to the airport, I had completely stopped crying and we boarded the plane and took our seats without incident. However, once the plane took off and I guess my mind began to consider what emotional state my extended family would be in when we arrived home, I wept uncontrollably. I tried to muffle the urge to scream at the top of my lungs, but persons around us on the plane looked puzzled because I was crying so long and so hard. I could not get control of myself, and I didn't want to. Josh leaned away from nestling me in his chest to tell a few passengers that we were going through a terrible tragedy. They understood and backed away, giving us all the space we needed to mourn. It was a three and a half hour flight from Denver to Flint. I looked out the window and kept weeping, and then fell back into Josh's arms and buried my head in his chest. I hadn't noticed how hard he was crying because I was totally absorbed in my pain

When we stepped off the plane, Josh's Dad met us at the airport. While the two men waited for the luggage to come around on the conveyer belt, I had an urgent need to go to the bathroom. I told Josh I would be right back and began to walk away. But after three steps, I was running to the bathroom, where I found an empty stall and locked the door. I staggered behind the locked bathroom door, deciding at last to try to relieve my full bladder. It would be a fairly long ride home, and who knows what I would find when we got there. Yes, this was a good time to go.

I sat down and tried hard to relieve myself. But I was unable to release anything from my body. Worse, I couldn't move to get up. I was literally paralyzed and couldn't even call for help. My body began to violently shake and I was stuck in that position. I tried to steady my body by touching the wall of the stall, but my body had begun to absorb the shock that my mind was facing. I got frightened, thinking I might not ever get back to Josh and his father. I might never see my mother and other relatives again because I might die right here in the airport bathroom. Try as I might, I was unable to get control of the situation.

Before I could muster up a solid scream for help, Josh came to the bathroom door and called my name. I heard him ask if anyone were in the bathroom, and no woman responded. So he came right in the ladies' room and asked me to please try to lean forward in order to unlock the stall I was sitting in. I actually strained my whole body to accomplish that simple task, and as the door began to swing open, Josh pushed it the rest of the way and embraced me forcefully and tenderly. Grief had overwhelmed me, and yet I sensed that Josh would be my fortress and my strength through this whole ordeal.

I could hardly walk, and just sank into his arms. This was going to be the beginning of the very long process of dealing with grief and the shock of our loss. When we got to his father's house, we heard all the details of the accident, and it appeared my Dad was at fault. What happened was that Dad thought he had room on the road to pass a slow moving vehicle, and he looked both ways before moving into the left lane and accelerating to get around the other car. However, another car was coming towards them, moving in the lane Dad and my family were driving in, and I guess the speed of both cars was sufficient that the cars collided at high speeds before Dad could find his way back into his lane of traffic, ahead of the vehicle he passed.

The fact that he was accelerating to get around the other car caused his speed to be higher than he would otherwise be driving, and the results were, predictably, that everyone in both cars would perish in the subsequent accident. That's exactly what happened. In that head on collision, the other father and son were also killed. My sister was just fifteen years old, and we lost our small poodle, that died in her arms. Not one person could focus on blaming Dad for anything at this terrible time, because we would have given anything for everyone to be alive, with me fussing at Dad for driving too fast and using poor judgment. God had not intervened, but He altered all our plans for what we could only perceive to be the worst thing in the world! I did pause momentarily to grieve for the persons in the other car, but my mind and heart and spirit were all centered on my immediate family, all gone in an instant. I was the only family member left, and all I wanted, when that realization hit me, was to die too.

I actually had no time then to truly grieve because there were three caskets to pick out, three sets of clothes to bring from Mom and Dad's home to the funeral parlor, and oh, God, three obituaries to prepare! There were insurance forms and an endless stream of papers needing to be found and signed and sent somewhere to be properly filed. I was in a whirlwind, which I realized later in life, saved me from losing my mind. I could easily have slipped into a depression from which I could not emerge, except for the volume of tasks that only I could complete.

Josh's Dad, and actually his whole family, couldn't do enough to make Josh and me as comfortable as possible. We would be sleeping there because it was too painful to go to my home and walk around the house that would forever be empty now. Still, we had to go there to get appropriate things for the funeral. Our first stop was the funeral home, where the three bodies of my family were being kept. Thankfully, the funeral director didn't ask if I wanted to view the bodies, so I was spared that incomprehensible action.

After we left the funeral home, we had to go to my house and find outfits in which to bury my dad, mom and sister. This was my first time going back into the house since the prior Christmas. It wasn't a question of whether or not I could enter the house without more than a couple of family members surrounding me. I needed support. So my aunt and husband and I went into the house, which was so still, as if the very walls knew that all the life had left the house. We moved slowly from room to room, seeing beds unmade and dishes in the sink. They must have left in a hurry because they never left the house like that. I wondered what made them late to my grandparents in the first place. That likely caused Dad to be rushing, and to make the regrettable decision to pass another car on the road.

We got to the dining room, and my mother had already purchased my birthday gifts, which were still unwrapped. It was the end of June, and my birthday was July 7th. I don't remember all the gifts that were spread across the dining room table, but my eyes fell upon a dress that Mom had picked out for me. It was tan, with beautiful, muted flowers on it. They were blues and greens and violets, and I thought about how much Mom knew my style and the colors that look good on me. There was a scoop neck with a tie in the front. It flowed straight down and came just above my knees, and I picked it up and held it against my body, as if Mom and I were in a department store together, laughing about the way the flowers caressed my figure.

I almost burst into tears right then, but instead, I made myself feel the calm pleasure of knowing Mom had picked it out for me. I carried it around for a while, and then I told my aunt I would wear this dress to the funeral because this is the last thing I will ever get from my Mom. I refused to wear black for this reason, on top of the fact that I had packed no black, or any other color dress in my haste to leave Colorado and get home to Michigan. The relatives, use to the Greek tradition of all the women wearing black to a funeral, did not protest my insistence upon wearing this particular dress. Mom never knew she would be leaving this earth on the day I was getting ready to wear this birthday dress. In retrospect, I realize that every time I wore that dress since the funeral, I always had a happy heart because my Mom purchased it for me before she died.

After we chose my dress, we went to bedrooms of my father, mother and sister, to select just the right clothing for each to wear at the funeral. My Dad had often told the family that he didn't want an open casket, with relatives who never visited now staring and saying stupid things about his appearance. I was determined, despite my enormous grief, to honor what I knew for certain my Dad wanted done upon his death. The thought of losing three of the "4 Ms" -- Michael, Marcella, Marcia and Maria – at the same instant, slammed against the back of my brain, causing a sharp pain to hit me in my head. My father was only fifty-three years old when he died. My mother was fifty-four.

This began a very laborious week. If you think a Greek wedding is something special, then you must attend at least one Greek funeral in your life! It's something that's a weeklong process. I believe I mentioned earlier that my father was VP, General Manager of a men's clothing store. He took great pride in the way he looked. My Dad did not have a will, so I was the only survivor at age twenty-one left to deal with this tragedy and the plethora of Greek relatives wanting to interfere, while at the same time honoring the wishes of my father.

My mother's sister and my family planned the funeral. The bodies needed to be prepared for burial, and I asked for closed caskets for all of them. It was a very bad accident and they would not have looked like themselves at all. Because I was spared from ever seeing my family again, my memory of the last time I saw them all alive was a happy one. Part of mourning, as I have learned over my life, is seeing people in a casket. That's part of closure. So some of my relatives were not happy. But they did respect my father's and my wish, and all caskets would be closed through the entire week of mourning and when they were lowered into the ground. Two of my uncles were in the funeral business, so they added their input, but I stayed out of all the details except the closed casket.

We planned to have a burial from that Tuesday to Saturday. For all that time, we just sat in the funeral home and watched people come and go. My sister was entering her junior year of high school, so her whole high school of students and staff turned out to support the family. I already spoke about how popular Dad was in our town, and Mom made her mark on the community as well. Then there was the very large, extended family. It may be morbid but none of them would miss being at the funeral home during the whole week leading up to the burial.

It was quite a sight to see. They ran out of flowers in all of Flint, Michigan! There was standing room only in the funeral home, which was devoted exclusively to our family. Normally, the funeral home served at least three grieving families. The number of people who would form a processional line from the funeral parlor to the gravesite would be enormous! God must have laid it on my parents' heart to have a portrait done that year – the only one done without me. So I still have a portrait of my parents and sister.

I learned something very interesting during this week of public mourning – something I will never forget. There are times when people wanting to offer comfort need to be silent. I say this because, when people die or experience great tragedy, unless we can relate on a very personal level, we should refrain from making statements like, *"This is God's will, honey."* I thought to myself, "This can't be God's will!!!!" *"God must have needed more roses in His garden."* I wanted to stand up and scream, "Why didn't he pick some of YOUR roses?" I felt combative and yet helpless. But mostly, I felt angry. I was angry with God, angry with my husband because he moved me far away from my family, and angry with my Dad because he made a decision behind the wheel of the car that caused the accident that took many lives. I found myself drifting into what I can say now was clinical depression.

But I have also realized that trying to offer words of comfort to me was people's way of grieving, too. But if you believe if it is God's will for people to die in horrific accidents, or by taking them through disease, then I say that is not my God. At that moment, something shifted in me because I became, in an instant, a person who refused to cry. I didn't want people to see my pain because they couldn't comfort me. But in doing that, I began to mask what I was truly feeling. I didn't realize that's what I was doing. Christian women in church are

34

supposed to be strong, so I decided I couldn't cry or feel really anything anymore. I am not sure why I felt this way, but the feeling was very real.

So while I sat at that funeral parlor from Tuesday to Friday, mechanically kissing more people than you could imagine, I withdrew from mainstream society and went to a dark place deep within my soul. Perhaps God saw that if I went much deeper, I'd never become all He had purposed for me to be, because on Friday night, something traditional turned into something incredibly humorous. This will be especially fun for my Greek readers. During a Greek funeral, the family must hire professional "wailers." They are the older members of the church, and they come and wail, often moving from standing to sitting to throwing themselves across caskets or falling to the floor. "Wailing" makes a very interesting sound. Many people that night had never, ever heard that sound before, including all of my husband's family and friends. It paralleled a bunch of chickens in a yard, running after a limited supply of seeds. It was like a cackle, not a chant or rhythmic prayer. You couldn't ignore wailers, nor could you hear yourself speak while wailers were in their glory. Just as we had an overflow of flowers and people food and cars, we had an excessive number of wailers for my Dad, Mom and sister!

The people in attendance that Friday evening were experiencing something funny. Try as you may to stay somber and respectful of the dead, you found yourself muffling laughter at the sight and sound of these wailers. I was no exception. My mood changed from the deepest depression and sadness to a fleeting moment of levity. And in a moment, I couldn't help myself and I began to laugh. It was contagious, and those around me laughed too, although embarrassed, burying our heads into our shoulders and looking like we were sobbing. As those nearest those of us in the front row cried in anguish for our misery, we laughed harder. I began to think how wonderful God is to bring us to a state of joy, even in this horrible circumstance. God gave me a glimmer of joy for the first time in my life, and I had the presence of mind to recognize it.

My family was buried that Saturday, after a very long church service. There were so many people in church and at the gravesite that the whole town was paralyzed with traffic. We said goodbye and left. When you finally get through a week of serious mourning, ending in a formal burial, you can begin to heal. I needed to begin to heal, but I didn't know how and nobody knew how to help me. I experienced days of utter loneliness, and neither Josh nor either of our extended families could afford me the peace I so desperately sought. I was alone to figure out how to get past this kind of loss. My world moved from stark contrasts of "black and white" to the "gray" that I saw from behind the mask I wore every waking moment of my life.

We stayed home for a full month, while I tried to figure out the moment it would be right for me to leave everything I had loved all my life, and return to my present existence. I was literally a "babe in Christ," and tried to bring to my consciousness the lessons about Jesus I had learned in my Colorado church. But all I could focus upon was the absence of God in my life, and in the whole universe! I had a terrible time discerning God's will. How do you discern God's will and stand on His promises, when your entire family, including your favorite pet, died in an instant? How? How!

During that period of time, I had lived eighteen years in the Greek Church and truly, I had never experienced any unnatural deaths. Everyone at all the funerals I attended died naturally. Nobody had died in a tragic accident. So I was crying out to God, "Why would

I want to continue to follow you? Why?" I longed for God to break through the heavens and give me an audible response that afforded me the comfort I absolutely needed. But He didn't do that. It's a slippery slope when we're very young Christians, and we think if we utter a question, God will respond the way our mate responds from across the breakfast table. We think we can walk out life alone, but we can't.

After being home for a month, we went back to Colorado and to church. And on that first Sunday, as much as people loved me and wanted to reach out to me, nobody knew what to say or how to help. I was convinced that nobody had experienced anything like I had. I went through the service almost in a trance. But as the congregation stood to sing the last hymn, something made me listen to every word of the song, *"Amazing Grace."* *"Amazing Grace, how sweet the sound that saved a wretch like me. I once was lost, but now am found, was blind, but now I see."* Tears began to stream down my cheeks because God was reminding me in that moment that it had only been a few years since I was lost – but now I was found. I was blind, and now I could see. And I knew beyond a shadow of doubt that my father, mother and sister left this earth knowing Jesus. They were in heaven, but the hard part was that I had to live on earth without them. And I didn't know how to do that. That part of the journey was, and has always been, the hardest.

Life went back to normal – actually we were living a "new normal" because not a day would pass that we didn't think of my family. I returned to work, but something would never ever be the same. A little portion of my heart had died on June 18, 1978. It was the beginning of a lot of pain I had yet to experience before I found my true place in God.

Chapter 2 Reflections:

1 Thessalonians 5:18 (NKJV):
"In everything give thanks; for this is the will of God in Christ Jesus for you."

Has something tragic happened to you that you feel you have been hanging onto? Are you angry or bitter toward God? Ask God to reveal any hidden anger, bitterness or un-forgiveness in you, and know God weeps with you in those painful life experiences. Write your thoughts on forgiveness here.

_____

_____

_____

_____

_____

_____

Chapter 3
Existing In The Dark

When we came back, our daily lives needed to resume. I had to go back to work, and he had to go back to school. It was his senior year. He was even more intent upon landing a "top ten" graduating position in his class because those students at the top of the class had the automatic access to the best jobs. Josh was always at the law library, from early morning to the middle of the night, and this was his habit almost every night. I felt so alone, so lonely, so far away from the God I had just learned to love. I fought off the mind battles that told me Josh was neglecting me, and tried to hear my father's voice in my ear telling me I would soon be "Mrs. Lawyer," and for that reason, I should bear all things and find a way to make myself content.

As I went to work every day, co-workers seemed to almost tip toe around me, like I was an upright piece of shattered glass, and they were waiting for the broken pieces to fall to the floor. I hated being pitied, and yet, neither my work friends nor I knew how to ease my pain. Everyone wanted to do and say the right thing, but when words failed, they resorted to moving around me silently and quickly, with their eyes looking towards the floor to avoid looking into my eyes. Grief is something no human being handles well, so by default, I was the one who had to make sense of it all because I was the grievant.

Unable and unwilling to show my emotions, I developed the perfect way to cope. I hid my misery behind a mask that made everyone around me breathe more easily. They assumed that my weak smile meant I had come through the worst and was on my way back to "normal." There would never again be a "normal" life for me, but I felt the obligation to make those around me feel better. Imagine that!

I went day after day, doing the ordinary tasks associated with my husband/wife relationship and my work relationship, as if I were a programmed robot with which the maker was pleased. While Josh found self-fulfillment in his studies and the bright future that awaited him as a lawyer, I went home daily to an empty house. Most evenings, Josh and I had dinner together, exchanging few words because there seemed nothing significant to talk about. Then, before I finished cleaning up the kitchen, he would return to the library to study. It was too early for me to go to bed, and because I wasn't in school, I had nothing to study – nothing that would keep my mind from going to a very dark place.

It was in the dark of the night that I found my mind wandering back to my childhood. I remembered vividly how I had those early nightmares of always being alone. I had the same dream almost nightly, where some catastrophe was separating me from my parents, and I was frantically trying to find them. The panic in my heart was so severe that I awoke, and then I used to run to my parents' bed and sleep between them. They always held me until I stopped trembling and fell asleep in their safe and loving arms. Even after my sister arrived six years after me, I continued to have dreams of being separated from my parents. I dreamed I was separated from my parents and my sister too – the three persons with whom I had the strongest bonds.

Because I had received nightly comfort and validation that I mattered much to my family, my young mind dismissed the nightmares each time they interrupted my sleep. How could I possibly realize God was giving me a premonition of what was coming?

Now, as I sat alone in my clean kitchen, allowing my mind to bring me back to those awful dreams, I felt all of the fear, but none of the comfort I had received so long ago.

I remembered how I never wanted to spend the night anywhere away from my parents. I used to pack my little suitcase with nightclothes, my toothbrush and my favorite toy, with no intentions of really staying the night. My parents knew it too. Even with my grandmother, who lived across the street, Mom would bring me to visit, after she and I talked about my desire to spend the night there. After we laughed and ate and played, Mom would say, *"Well, it's time for me to go and my little Marcia to stay with Grandma. Goodbye, and I'll see you in morning."* She would kiss me and I would kiss her as if we were separating. Then, as she walked out the door, I would kiss my Grandma, pick up my unopened suitcase and follow right behind my Mom. It happened every time. It was as if, as a small child, I knew my days with my parents would be numbered.

The only exception to that was when I visited my Auntie Kaye. She was Mom's sister, and from the time I was born, she always doted over her first niece and loved me dearly. She was a person of comfort for me, and her home was a place where I experienced unconditional love. She was more than my Auntie Kaye. She was my second mother. Only with her did I actually spend the night, and I slept as soundly as if I were positioned between my two parents. I even had my own bed, with a yellow chenille bedspread that had little puffballs that made a beautiful design over every inch of the soft, pretty spread.

Many times, Auntie Kaye stepped in when my Dad decided to discipline me. She would defend my rights as a teenager, as she always softened the sting of whatever Dad was about to say or do to me. My Uncle Dick was as much a part of my early happiness as Auntie Kaye. As a matter of fact, they later became Grandma and Grandpa to my children. I leaned heavily on both of them when my family died so suddenly. They truly were my second parents, eagerly willing to step into the role vacated by my parents, if I needed them to do so.

Life is so interesting, or maybe I should say God is so good, because He allowed my mind to go from the fear of separation from my parents to the happiness I felt with my "second parents." However, I had so much alone time while my husband was studying law, that one night of happy memories of my childhood and teen years was quickly replaced the next night by a flood of dark memories about losing my entire nuclear family. I had become painfully aware that my phone would no longer ring on Sundays, where I looked forward to long conversations with, first Dad, then Mom, and finally Maria. My anchor was missing, and I was floundering in the ocean with no land in sight. Josh saw none of this in my eyes or in my demeanor because I had quickly mastered the art of wearing a mask from the time I awoke to the time I closed my eyes at night. I thought I had everything under control.

I tried each day to keep my mind from going into what I now know is "clinical depression." I focused on my physical surroundings and my home furnishings. We had my parents' furniture moved from Michigan to our place in Boulder, Colorado. Those cement walls containing two sparse pieces of art were now full with visual memories of the lives of my family during my entire growing up. It added warmth to my otherwise cold living space. When I sat on the soft couch or the big armchair Dad used to love, I could feel my family around me, and I temporarily regained the comfort of crawling into my parents' bed.

Actually, the best "pain remedy" was my *Baldwin Acrosonic* piano. This was the inanimate object that used to come to life every time my family gathered around it. I had taken piano lessons for four years, and after all that time and expense, I was an enthusiastic pianist with the talent of a drummer. I banged out *Chopin's* melodies in a way that would surely make him "turn over in his grave," as they say. But my playing, and the supportive energy from my family listening to each performance piece, brought a unique joy to our household for years. When I felt that deep depression trying to overtake me, especially at night, when I was home alone, I often ran to the piano and started playing my part of the famous duets I used to play with Mom. The most popular, of course, were *"Chopsticks"* and *"Heart and Soul!"* Any melody would have been sufficient to silence the screams emanating from the depth of my soul.

So here it was in my home with my parents' furniture and my memories nailed to the cement walls, sitting alone while my husband pursued his law degree. In an instant, depression overtook me once more because Mom wasn't there, sitting next to me on the piano bench. I cringed at the thought that never again would our elbows touch, as we giggled and played the song a little faster. My sister, Maria, who walked in and out of the room where her sister and mother thought themselves to be master pianists, was basically disinterested in our upward climb to performing in *Carnegie Hall.*

Suddenly, my focus shifted to my little sister, who would never come to see me again. She was just fifteen when she died. She would never grow up to marry or have children, and we could never talk together about our offspring and mates and careers. Our kids would never play together as we mused about the time when we were the kids. I found myself sobbing into my hands with no tissue in sight. We had just begun to have a real sisterly relationship when Maria died. How tragic, and how cruel of a merciful God to take her from me this way! My pain grew, as my faith diminished until faith left me altogether.

I didn't realize it at the time, but it would be in this darkness that I began to resent my husband, Josh. He took me away from my family, and the first ugly thing I remembered on one of the earliest evenings when I was all alone was that little *Pizza Hut* in Kansas City, where he said he wanted to see if I would really leave my father. That sentence haunted me well beyond the fact that I couldn't finish my meal that evening. It was mean and selfish, and I thought it unnecessary because I was raised to follow my husband, so of course I would leave my father for my husband. But truthfully, I never wanted to be separated from my parents. I always wanted to figuratively be in their bed, in the middle of them, feeling safe and protected as I slept. In the natural, however, I saw no reason why I couldn't live dutifully with my husband and still be near my very close family. I couldn't have that because my husband, Josh, had taken me far, far away from them for his own selfish reasons.

I was drowning at just twenty-two years old. I decided to take an English class at the *University of Colorado*. I needed to fill my mind with lectures of professors, and not memories of the dead. It was during this time that, somewhere inside me, I felt that being a student again was fun. I was not headed for any particular degree, so I basically could enjoy the experience of college. As the months passed, I began to see myself doing better and better, and I honestly thought that when Josh graduated from law school, I might have the opportunity to pursue a college degree. After all, I had worked hard to put him through law school, and he would be making a hefty salary soon. Surely, he would think it a great idea to put me through college, especially if I did well in my first course.

It was time for my final, and it had been years since I took this kind of a test. I studied relentlessly, and then it was time. The professor handed out the exams, and I remember getting the final exam and immediately glancing through the pages. It looked to be a long exam. Nevertheless, much to my surprise, I finished the test, and when I closed the test booklet, I felt I had truly accomplished the task and earned a good grade. It was several days before I received my grade. Not only did I pass, but also I received the highest "A "grade among 50 students! I could not wait to run to the law library to share with Josh my great accomplishment because I knew how happy he would be hearing my news.

When I got to his study group, it was obvious that they could not be disturbed. I sat down next to him and quietly whispered my awesome news of getting the highest grade in the class on the final exam. I asked quietly if we could leave the library and celebrate with French fries and a *Coke*. He looked at me coldly and said he had no time to participate in my celebration. How could I have been so wrong about his reaction to my wonderful news? How could I have been so wrong about the man I chose to be my husband for life? I got up, dejected, and with my head down and my heart lower, I returned once more to an empty house to share this news with nobody. Boy did I miss my family now. If there was a seed of resentment before, I could say I hated him at that point on that night. I didn't have Dad anymore to remind me that it would all work out in the end.

At this moment, I felt certain that it was never going to work out. There was no one for me to share my success with, or to appreciate the self-doubt that preceded my even signing up for the course. My confidence was high now, and I believed I could go from having a "Mrs. Degree" to a real college degree. I could be a significant wage earner and a definite helpmate to Josh. Why didn't he see that? I had fallen in love with a shallow, self-absorbed man, and worse, I had worked like a dog in a menial job to put him through law school.

I felt like my heart would burst if I didn't celebrate, so I called a co-worker and asked him to meet me at a *Denny's* for that *Coke* and fries that Josh couldn't be bothered having with me. The friend hugged me and congratulated me. As we raised our two glasses of *Coke* in a toast to my mental acumen, I felt validated and worthy. It didn't come from my husband, who was too busy being engaged in "important" work to find my little top-of-the-class "A" notable. As my friend said goodbye to me, giving me a gentle kiss on my forehead, he said in a voice that sounded like the famous actor, Humphrey Bogart, *"Here's lookin' at you, kid!"*

Josh and I never brought my success up again, but focused exclusively upon his finals and graduation. He would be a lawyer, and he would meet his personal goal of graduating among the top ten in his class. I like to think part of his success was that I worked to support us, and he had the freedom to study with his group without having to think about the day-to-day household operation. Good thing I didn't just fall apart and wring my hands in defeat when my whole family perished. I was certainly entitled to a breakdown, but I found the inner strength to keep going. Josh benefited from this, but neither of us acknowledged this non-insignificant fact.

Chapter 3 Reflections:
Psalm 120:1 (NKJV):
"In my distress I cried to the Lord, and he heard me."

Are you living in the dark? When you feel you are in darkness, keep crying out with the knowledge that your Lord hears you! Remember it is ok to not be ok. The one who holds the world together holds you, too! Take a few minutes to pour your heart out to God.

_____

_____

_____

_____

_____

_____

Chapter 4
Moving Forward To Go Backward

Once Josh finished law school with such a high class ranking, he had to sit for the Bar examination in Colorado. We never planned to return to Michigan, first because we both loved Colorado. But also, I could never return to Michigan, with my parents and sister gone forever. While he was preparing for the Bar exam, he was also planning a month-long trip to celebrate graduation and to bring some joy back into my life. The death of my family had taken its toll on me and on our marriage. I would describe Josh's attitude at that time to be somewhere between loving and attending to me, and being the macho man taking the lead in planning a vacation we BOTH needed. Now that graduation was behind him, he had time to see me and realize I was hurting, not healing.

We needed to spend some time getting to know each other all over again. During our four short years of marriage, he was buried in books and I worked every day. He sat and passed everything, and now had a job lined up. He was driven, even though finding a job was no problem for him. It would be in Denver, Colorado, and we signed a lease, with the expectation that we would move when we returned from this essential trip.

Josh's trip sounded like a great idea. I quit my job, and didn't line up a job before we left. My kind of job would always be available. I never went back to college, but the seed of academic success was planted in my brain and on my heart.

We owned a CJ-5 Jeep that we would take on this journey, and our month long trip would be filled with sightseeing. We booked no hotels before we left, but just took off. Our first stop would be in Yuma, Arizona, to visit and stay with Auntie Kaye and her family. She greeted us with deep hugs and kisses, laughing about the fact that the only place I would actually spend the night as a child was her home. We stayed four days, during which time her boys, my Uncle Dick and Josh spent lots of fun hours in the sand dunes of Arizona, riding our jeep over much hilly terrain. Auntie and I stayed back and caught up on life. We were both still grieving, but being together gave us time to talk and process what life had become without Michael, Marcella and Maria. I was first granddaughter, niece, and child in the family – the first! My mother was a nervous mother and Auntie was calm. She was the baby of my mother's family, and she had a way about her of calming Mom when she insisted on staying in her nervousness. My Auntie Kaye made Mom acknowledge that it was Auntie who held me and quieted me as an infant. I can't describe how much we bonded over the years, but we were extremely close.

After four days, it was time to leave Auntie Kaye and Uncle Dick. Next stop on our trip was San Diego. Josh and I had "fun in the sun" on the beach and driving up the coast and staying at hotels or motels along the way. It was kind of romantic that we booked nothing because we were young and the world belonged to us. Our end point would be Alberta, Canada, where Josh and his other nine siblings were born. We would be driving to Oregon, Washington State, British Columbia and Banff National Park. The beauty of the scenery along every road on this trip was astounding, breathtaking, however, our marriage was better. We had this time that we had lost, and we were spending time together. I never spoke to Josh about my growing resentment towards him because there was always a chance that this trip would bring back the love that had been pushed out of my heart as resentment and bitterness crept in. I was finding my husband again to be that person who helped me through the biggest crisis of my life. He was my rock. The sweetness of married life began to return, but it would be short-lived.

Upon arriving in Alberta, Canada, we stayed with some of his family friends, arriving on a bright, sunny Saturday. That Sunday, we decided to take this family on a ride in Quaker Country, which I had never seen. I wasn't sure if this family was related to Josh, or dear friends of his family. So I thought of them as "the man and his wife, and the teen daughter and young son."

We were all excited about the outing before us, except the older daughter, who stayed behind. This gentleman and I bantered playfully about who would sit in the front passenger seat where I had sat during the whole journey to that point. I wanted to sit there because it was my place. He had never ridden in an open jeep before, and he wanted the two men to sit together in the front seat to enjoy the scenery of the beautiful Canadian mountains. The air was fresh and crisp. I relented and sat in the back with the boy and the man's wife. They were the sweetest, most loving people, so none of us was unhappy about the seating arrangement because we were in for a day of fun. Our plan was to spend a few days here in Canada, after which we would drive down to Montana, Wyoming, and finally to Colorado to pack up our old place and move to the new one near Josh's new job with a prestigious law firm.

We were driving on a dirt road, traveling about 25 miles an hour. We crested a small hill, and as we came down the other side, we hit some gravel, and

Josh lost control of the vehicle. I felt the back end swivel sideways before the jeep flipped over. Everything moved in slow motion, and I could feel myself screaming, but couldn't hear the screams. I could feel the fishtailing of the back end of the jeep, and that's the last thing I remember until an hour later when I was wandering aimlessly in a field. I faintly heard my name being called, and it was Josh lying on the ground calling for me. I was so dazed that I couldn't recall how I found my way to him, but I did. As I bent over to talk to him, I felt pain in my mouth and realized I had lost my front two teeth. I saw scratches and cuts on him that didn't look life-threatening, but he didn't want to move, so I knew something else was wrong. He drew me closer to him as if to either gain strength from touching me, or to take his last breath and leave me like my parents and sister did.

I heard a paramedic calling out for us. He rushed over, quickly looked at me, and noted that I had teeth missing, but appeared to have no other injuries. They put a neck brace on my husband, moved him onto a board because they couldn't get a stretcher down to that field where they found us. They carried him to the ambulance, as he cried out in severe pain.

I followed him to the ambulance, where we met the wife and her son. Oh, God! I had forgotten about this other family while I was wrapped up in Josh's condition and my mouth. Now I forced myself to focus on them. Neither the mother nor her son had any injuries, but we were told that her husband had been killed instantly. He and I had wanted the front passenger seat, and he was the one who ended up there. I had given up my seat to my new friend. I don't remember seeing the body, but clearly I was in shock. So the deceased husband may have been lying right near my feet.

There were only lap belts and no shoulder harnesses back then, so when the jeep rolled over, the husband's head hit the ground before the roll bar did, and he died of massive head injuries. I had "survivor's remorse," immediately feeling guilty for being alive while this poor man died. In this moment, I couldn't process what we were being told. I believe in retrospect that my mind could not comprehend or accept one more fatality in the short time since my family died.

I don't remember the reason, but I was not in the ambulance with my husband going to hospital. This woman and her son would have to go home to tell the daughter that her father was dead – just like that! This was a family I didn't know until I met them a day previously, and once more, I'm surrounded by death. I wanted to scream at the top of my lungs, "God, why had I really sat in the back and not the front? Why have you spared my life and taken this innocent man's life? Are you trying to push me completely away from You?" God didn't answer me and I was furious about that, too.

The minute we got to their house, I called Josh's mother, who knew this family well, and I said, "You've got to come." I thought I sounded completely incoherent, but I must have made enough sense for her to arrive the next day. Meanwhile, I had to get to the hospital to see about Josh. I didn't know what was wrong with him in terms of the extent of his injuries. The hospital was over an hour away, and yet members of this family who had just lost a father and husband took me to visit Josh. It turned out that he had a broken collarbone, broken neck with no paralysis, thankfully, and internal injuries. He would live. My husband would live, but this woman's husband would never spend another moment with her. It was so unfair!

A physician in the emergency room took a look at my mouth and noted that I had no dirt around my mouth, which would indicate that I probably didn't lose the teeth by hitting my face on the pavement. No, they were fairly certain that I hit my teeth on the roll bar as the jeep was flipping over. The whole hour I was wandering in that field remained a blur to me, and to this day, I have no memory of that part of the accident. I may have walked to the body or seen it, but I have no memory of that hour at all.

All five of us were thrown from the vehicle, and we sustained one fatality and one injured person with a couple of missing teeth. My front teeth had hit something so hard that I had broken the teeth down to the nerve. I would be getting temporary crowns that Monday, while waiting for my mother-in-law to arrive. These were her best friends, and here Josh and I were right in the middle of all the uncertainty and chaos. It had only been one year and two months and a day since the death of my family. I don't remember, but I don't believe I cried. I was in shock. I remember thinking, "What's in my life that I need to fix? What's in my life, God?" I was still crying out to a God I had perceived to be very angry with me, but I was angrier than I had ever experienced in my life. What? What? What do I need to do to stop this madness!

My mother-in-law came right away, and we began walking out the long process of Josh's healing. He was in tremendous pain. The jeep was totaled in an accident no one could have controlled. We had screwed around in that jeep the whole distance, and never before did the jeep leave the road. It was a freak happening, nobody was at fault. It only flipped once and came back up on its tires, but it was too late. That single flip of the vehicle caused a single death.

We had to wait a month before Josh was healed enough to leave Canada and return to the USA. My mother-in-law was so good to me; so loving and kind at a time when I was completely vulnerable. She was my Mom, taking care of me when I went to the hospital.

Josh got home just in time for the gentleman's funeral. I wanted my mother-in-law to stay longer, but she explained she had to leave because she was emotionally exhausted and had to return to work. I stayed a month with the woman who became a new widow, and with her children, who needed someone to help them process their grief and loss. All of them were in shock.

For weeks we stayed at her home waiting for medical clearance to be able to drive home. I felt so guilty getting into bed with my husband and this poor woman, our host, was going to bed alone. We were devastated that our lives had been spared and we could hear her crying. I was still grieving, and now we added grief of loss for family Josh had known growing up.

I could not reconcile in my own mind that I was here and he was not. If I died, I could be with my parents and sister in paradise. I didn't know what to do to stop the tremendous guilt from overtaking me.

I had no understanding of what God intended to teach me. I didn't understand any of that. So this part of my life would again fuel the anger I had been carrying for over a year. It fueled the bitterness -- that sense of not understanding who God was. Why would this happen one year, two months and one day after He took my whole family? I believed He took those people from me too. And I began to believe that the God I had given my life to was out to get me, and I better duck and look behind me at every turn. That is how I felt, and I began to walk out those feelings in my life.

We just wanted to go home. This was more than we could handle. When he was medically released, we left and had to fly home. We had no transportation, as the Jeep had been totaled. During the extended time we were in Canada, we had to be out of student housing at college, so friends did the packing and moving for us. I saw Christian brotherhood like I had never seen it before. Those friends formed a team, packed and cleaned and moved us all the way to Denver.

I had been living in such a "Why Me?" mentality, but God was starting to turn back the edge of the curtain for me to glimpse the same kind of his Godly love that I had seen when these church friends brought us airline tickets to get back to Michigan right after my family died. I was too distraught to recognize the selfless love then. These same people stepping in again to rescue us at a time when we were helpless, injured, and hurting beyond the physical pain of having been involved in another fatal accident. I began to see God's hand in my truly messed up world.

Chapter 4 Reflections:
Psalm 23: 1-4 (NKJV):
"The LORD is my shepherd; I shall not want. He makes me to lie down in green pastures; He leads me beside the still waters. He restores my soul; He leads me in the paths of righteousness for His name's sake. Yea, though I walk through the valley of the shadow of death, I will fear no evil; For You are with me; Your rod and Your staff, they comfort me."

Has your life been filled with what seems like endless pain? If so, meditate on this scripture. Study the role of an earthly shepherd, and see Jesus in the role of your heavenly shepherd. Quiet your mind, take a breath and allow Jesus to comfort you. Write down your cares and concerns, and then try to give them over to your heavenly shepherd.

Chapter 5
Living On A Slippery Slope

The couple from our church that had taken the lead in moving us from Boulder to Denver, Colorado also picked Josh and me up at the airport. We were heading to a place in which we had never lived, and we didn't know if our furniture would be leaning against walls. We had no idea where things either were, or had yet to be placed. Mind you, we were humbly grateful for all that had been done for us, but we wondered about the task ahead. Josh was still healing from the broken collarbone and broken neck, his internal injuries were pretty much healed. Still, he was incapable of doing any lifting or moving.

When we walked into our new home, we were elated to see that all the furniture had been arranged in a way that we could enjoy our new surroundings. In the kitchen were the boxes our friend, Denise, felt couldn't be unpacked for us because they didn't know how we might want the kitchen set up. The same was true for the bathroom. Our lovely piano was in the center of the living room, and Denise told us that this heavy instrument had to be professionally lifted from the ground to the third floor where we lived. My, my, how much our church friends loved us! We couldn't thank them enough, for extending themselves so far for us. Denise just smiled.

Fortunately, we had a second vehicle, so transportation was not an immediate issue for us. Over the next couple of weeks, Josh rested and did what he could to put the rest of the apartment together. But most of the heavy lifting literally fell to me.

Josh's new law firm was patiently waiting for him to get well, and he felt comforted that a quality job awaited him. After all those long nights in law school, he was joining a prestigious firm, and he had a bright future ahead of him. I, on the other hand, was perusing the Classified Ads in the newspapers for positions that interested me. I had limited education, so my choices were limited too. I found something that caught my eye – Administrative Assistant to the Vice President of a firm of surgical technologists whose job was vital to doctors in an operating room. My duties would include clerical work, support to the Vice President in constructing by-laws, and helping to organize their annual conference, which was set to take place in Denver.

I interviewed for this position, wearing my "Sunday best," and I was hired on the spot. It was a great feeling to be hired so quickly. This brought me back to the day I passed that course final with the highest "A" in the class. I had worth, and I was bright! There were no cell phones at that time in our lives, so I had to wait for Josh to come home that evening before I could share my good news. We needed both incomes because we had student loan debts to repay. Remember, he refused to take any money from my Dad.

When my family died, neither my Dad nor my mother had a will. Since I was the only survivor, I would have inherited several hundred thousand dollars. However, without a will, the entire estate went into probate. That meant that we would wait an undetermined amount of time for the disposition of the assets. Meanwhile, Josh and I were living in the leanest years of our lives, despite him being that lawyer my Dad talked about early in my marriage. The irony struck me keenly. My Dad had said for me to remain patient and obedient, sacrificing my schooling for Josh's. Deep down, I knew I had the ability to do so much more academically than to become "Mrs. Lawyer." But I valued everything Dad said, so I followed his plan. The one course I took told me I could easily earn a college degree and beyond. But my world was Josh's world, which meant I was finding a job in the Classified Ads, instead of having a headhunter find a top-notch position for me. The good news was that I was immediately marketable, and so I looked forward to my first day as an Administrative Assistant.

During all this flux between chaos and order, we had neglected to find a new church home. Like so many people, we vowed to do that "one day soon." But days turned into weeks and we got further from a church, and further from God. We got caught up in the busyness of life on top of still being in mourning for my family and the family we knew when the second tragic accident occurred. We both kept figuratively looking over our shoulder, telling God we were through with sadness and grief. We also told God how disappointed and saddened we were by our circumstances. Josh had been a Christian longer than I, so he was rooted in faith more strongly than I was. In my frail, and ignorant mind, I felt that if we didn't get back to God, it was just fine with me. Josh didn't challenge me on my negative thinking, but I could sense that if I were willing, he would find a church.

We had been married only four years to this point, and we had lived a lifetime of sorrow. This kind of loss is the stuff that breaks good marriages apart. We were unaware that anything contrary to our marriage for life could happen to us. It was at this time that I began to long for a baby. I thought hard about this idea because Josh had just begun his career. If I had a baby, I would have to stop working, and he would have to support now three people.

I began to share with Josh how I was feeling. It seemed like it was time for a child. He, coming from a large family, did not put up a fight. We agreed to stop all birth control, much to my surprise. Each month thereafter, we would wait to see if my menstruation cycle returned, and it always did. I used to cry because I wondered if God were punishing me for something by not allowing me to have a child. Every month that I wasn't pregnant, I began to turn my emotions inward. I continued to question God for taking my whole family, and for taking a husband of a family who knew me. Not getting pregnant just added to the pile of complaints I had against Father God.

While one day turned into another, and life continued, regardless of my level of depression, I threw myself into my job. I wore a mask that I carefully put on each day so that no one could see my tears. No one could see anything except a positive, smiling and gracious woman ready to do the day's work. My boss and I had a respectable relationship, and he was pleased with my work. However, the President of the company took an unhealthy interest in me at a time when my moral guard and self-worth were at the lowest point in my life. All of my self-esteem was coming from the job, with no gratification afforded me in my personal or married life.

Probably because I didn't have a church, and the related fellowship that comes from worshiping with other believers, I lost my focus on God, including the ability and will to pray throughout the day. I moved myself far away from God, without realizing that He never stopped loving me and chasing after me.

Void of correct reasoning about all that had happened to me over the last two years, I saw my husband in a different light. He was the one who brought me to church and to God. I fell in love with Jesus through Josh. My happiness as a "babe in Christ" was short-lived because the sadness came rushing in like a flood. Somehow, I blamed Josh for God failing me. Of course, I blamed God the most for that, but Josh was not off the hook in my delicate mind.

I twisted reality to reveal that my family died because my husband took me far away from them. This other family suffered the loss of its father because Josh was driving at the time. Now, I desperately wanted a child, and the only way to achieve that was through Josh, my husband. But that was not working out. Josh was in the middle of everything bad that had happened to me. I didn't see all this at the time, but my feelings had turned from love and affection to contempt. We moved through daily life like robots, leaving me empty enough to seek affection and validation outside our home.

Part of my job responsibility was planning for the annual conference in Denver, which put me directly in the company of the President. As we worked together on the project, we had to go to a meeting at the hotel where the three-day conference would be held. Afterwards, he took me to breakfast, letting me know of his great interest in me, despite knowing that I was married. You would think I would be offended, but I was immensely flattered. I had only dated one guy in high school before marrying Josh, so now here was this handsome, successful stranger courting me.

I left his presence, declining his invitation. But all the way home, I entertained the idea of what it would feel like to be with someone besides my husband, giving me personal and sexual attention. The fantasies that filled my head had become monsters around me by the time I reached my home. Fighting those voices of lust and pleasure was my Dad's single voice reminding me to hang in there because my marriage would eventually bring me the fulfillment I sought.

Before I stepped out of my car to join my husband in the apartment, I had to reconcile these competing spirits. Was there a way for me to keep my marriage, while satisfying my fantasy for a relationship outside my marriage? Of course not! But, there was a way, and it dropped right into my spirit as if being directed there. I could ask my husband for a separation, so we could both figure out who we were. During my separation, I would be living alone, and free to come and go at will. There would be the time and place for me to explore this other set of feelings that had taken over my immediate thought processes. It was a perfect plan!

The moment I entered my apartment, I decided I had to tell Josh right away that I wanted a temporary separation. He was shocked. Once he composed himself, he was willing for us to separate while I found whatever peace I was searching for. In fact, he gave me direction about how to set myself up in an apartment instructed me of things I should be sure to do in separating from him. We both cried because this was a really difficult decision for both of us. He had been my everything since I was in high school. The only condition he placed on my leaving was that, while I was trying to figure out where I fit into this life, both of us would abstain from extra-marital relationships. I readily agreed, knowing in my heart that I would never keep the promise I was making.

I had no problem telling Josh what I wanted to take when I moved, which would be just a couple of weeks from that moment. He, however, made up two lists. The first was all the things Marcia wanted. The second was all the things Marcia would get. He made the final decision, since he wasn't the one asking for the separation. I accepted the verbal terms Josh had set because I assumed we would be back together again within a few months. I never wanted a divorce, but I craved excitement and freedom from pain and depression. Thus, I accepted the twin bedroom set from the guest bedroom, some dishes and utensils, and my clothes. Basically, I was taking what I could carry out. We both knew that in the remote instance where this arrangement became permanent through a divorce, I would need furniture. But for now, I was prepared to sit on the floor and eat Sunday dinner.

Within a week, I found an apartment down the street from Josh. The moving commenced, with the help of a couple of girlfriends. There was some sort of sick excitement that this move brought me. All my creature comforts were with Josh, but my twin bed was my childhood bed. So that brought me comfort.

Back at the job, I was now ready to make it known to the President of the company that I had separated from my husband. I knew this would further his interest in me. And as we continued to plan for the upcoming conference, we worked late hours. Before we knew it, we were sneaking kisses, and all of a sudden, all my pain seemed to drift to a place in my mind that I could tuck away while I lived in the moment. This was the first time in my life that I can remember "*waiting to exhale.*" It felt right.

When the preparation for the conference was completed, the President insisted that all employees connected to the conference remain in the hotel overnight in case their assistance was needed. I readily agreed to stay at such a magnificent place, feeling instantly that here, I would be void of all the pain and stress at my home. All was going extremely well. Then, on the second night of our stay, I heard a knock at my hotel door. I knew before I looked through the keyhole that the President was standing outside. I went to the door with anxious anticipation. There he was standing with a bottle of champagne and a tray of strawberries. He was much older than I was. It was almost like I had plotted this moment. There was no voice in my ear from my Dad. I had no thoughts about Josh being alone tonight. My total focus was on this older, attractive, polished man before me. It was in this moment that the promise I made to Josh about never being unfaithful while we were separated would be broken.

Because we were working together, it was important for this man to leave and not spend the night. Others were at the conference, and we didn't want to be discovered. I knew in my spirit that what I had done was wrong, but all I felt was exhilaration, despite being fully aware that I had done something wrong. I guess the strongest sense I felt was comfort. I was getting lost in something that had nothing to do with the rest of my life. There was no memory in this brief union between two people of all the unthinkable things that had happened before. Deep down, I believe that the pain was so unbearable that I almost craved an outlet, albeit an affair with someone I knew from work – my boss, yet!

When I awoke the next morning, there was a call from the front desk saying I had a visitor in the front lobby. I had no idea who it could be, so I finished dressing for the conference and went downstairs to find Josh standing there. I'm sure I was visibly shaken to see him looking at me, and my guilt caused me to be certain that he knew what had transpired the previous evening. That meant he also knew that I had broken our marriage vows after promising to keep them sacred, despite our separation.

I slowly walked towards him, almost like a child ready to receive the punishment a parent intended to give out after something terrible that the child had just done. I was trying to keep calm, but my mind was too troubled to focus. Before I could either confess my sin or offer some small talk, Josh said in a calm voice, *"I wanted to surprise you. I know we said we would separate for a while, but I thought I would come and be with you this morning, like we always did when we had something to celebrate."* "Celebrate?" I asked with not the slightest idea of what we could possibly be celebrating. Josh looked dejected now, and he said, *"Don't you remember, it's my birthday."*

I was searching for a possible reason for me to have forgotten this important day, and I found a weak answer in the fact that I was busy with the conference. He accepted my limp excuse, just as I mustered up the sweetness to say, "Happy Birthday, Josh." Truthfully, the conference was all day and there was no time for me to leave for a quick bite or cup of coffee. So the words I believe he said were to the effect that we would postpone the birthday celebration. I was determined to stay separated and not let his tender look or words distract me from my desire to be single and on my own.

The conference ended the following day, and my boss and I returned to a professional mode, as if nothing personal or intimate had transpired between us just a night or so before. Because I was completely engrossed in my needs, it's no wonder that I neither sought nor found God, even for a brief prayer of confession. Therefore, I missed seeing the brazen signs of Satan, who took advantage of my vulnerability and made me believe completely that "the grass was greener" anywhere except in my home with my husband.

In retrospect, I sincerely believe that had I sought professional counseling after the first devastating accident where I lost my whole family, and then experienced another tragic death soon after, I would not have been such an easy mark for Satan. God would have met me and given me the spiritual tools to fight what I'll accurately call "clinical depression."

I knew nothing about "spiritual warfare," where Christians wearing the full armor of God actually war in the spirit to change something Satan has ordered to be done. As my life was about to take a series of twists and turns, I would learn that spiritual warfare was absolutely real.

A new week began after the conference and I went to work daily. Josh called me, but with each call, I had less to say and was quick to end the call. At the same time, my boss and I were flirting in the break room, brushing past each other in hallways, delighted at the avoidance of discovery, as we became more and more desirous of each other's flesh. We were very good at hiding our desires, even though both of us knew it was just a matter of time before we would find ourselves alone together. Satan is excellent at presenting the "tease" that traps us in the sin where we can't escape. I fell prey to the desires of the flesh, all to the delight of Satan. I would soon discover sin takes you further than you want to go, keeps you longer than you want to stay and costs you more than you want to pay!

My boss and I began spending nights together at his home, although I always woke before dawn and went home to shower and dress at my own place. What we did, however, was spend weekends together. I began leaving articles of clothing at his place for our mutual convenience.

It wasn't long before my immediate boss called me in and confronted me about the affair with our boss. He asked me if there was something going on between me and our boss. I immediately spoke up and said, "Yes." I realized instantly that my job could be in jeopardy, but I didn't want to lie to him out of genuine respect. He told me that he felt nobody else knew of our flirting, which was a relief. But he added that he would be speaking to our boss about the situation too, before things got out of hand and everyone was talking about us. I gave my boss my most remorseful face, as I lied and promised to be discreet. I never promised to end what would become a full-blown affair. I appreciated the fact that my boss had no condemnation in his voice, and maybe that gave me the devilish courage to both lie to him and more vigorously pursue the forbidden relationship.

Shortly after my immediate superior respectfully confronted our boss and me about the situation, the boss and I decided to tone things down at work, and enjoy each other's company in the evenings and on weekends. Josh knew that all my girlfriends were in Boulder, Colorado, so he couldn't understand how I could be away from the phone so often that I couldn't pick up late at night and early in the morning. Where could I be, if not in my place during those hours? I was, of course, in the arms and bedroom of my boss.

Every time I returned home, I checked my answering machine to find that Josh had called several times, during odd hours. I started to think of a response to the question he was sure to ask. "Where was I?" My husband was a lawyer who graduated tenth in his class, so I knew in my heart that he must have figured out that I had betrayed my promise to remain faithful when I stated that I wanted a separation. A kind of fear gripped me. On one hand, I told myself I was a grown woman, living on my own and not accountable to anyone. On the other hand, though, I must have had feelings for my husband, and I had grown up with a strong set of values. So I felt some responsibility to tell the truth. I ended the conversation with myself by saying that only if Josh brought up the truth would I acknowledge it.

One day, Josh called me and I answered. He was determined to confront me. He said, *"I know something's wrong because you're never home. It's time we had a face-to-face talk, and I'm asking you to come over now."* I was incredibly nervous, knowing the moment of truth was about to be revealed. I threw some clothes on and drove to our apartment. I had a key, but chose to knock so that Josh would open it. This was the first time I had been there since we separated.

There were no affectionate touches or words between us, but we were civil. Josh asked me plainly, *"Is there somebody else? Are you seeing another man?"* With the same honesty as I had displayed to my superior at work, I acknowledged that I was seeing my boss after hours and on weekends. All of the pigment left his face, and he was pale. He just shook his head in bitter disappointment. *"We had an agreement and you broke it. Does our marriage mean anything to you? Are you the least bit interested in saving it?"* I was thoroughly shamed. Everything he said was pure truth.

I acknowledged that I loved him still, and said I made a mistake. Josh was crying because I had deeply wounded him, and he was facing for the first time the fact that our marriage might be over. I was crying, saying very few words in response. I was guilty, and that was the end of it. As I stood there staring at Josh, I felt some perverse pleasure in his pain because my mind brought me right back to that *Pizza Hut* in Kansas, where Josh said he took me several states away from my beloved parents to see if I really would leave them. Here was my chance to inflict on him the kind of pain I felt when my family died. Deep inside me, I blamed him for the accident, which I had made myself believe happened because he took me so far away from home.

The benefits of professional counseling that we so badly needed, but never received, would have made the critical difference in what Josh and I were experiencing at this very moment. I daresay this would have saved our marriage. I was quickly brought back to reality when Josh said, *"It's evident that Satan has got you in his grip. You are not the girl I married. And I want to end the marriage right now."* Josh said we should each take a couple of weeks to get our thoughts together before we formally filed papers for a divorce. As sad as I was about the dissolving of our marriage, I was relieved in that moment that the truth was out. I could stop living in two worlds. Had my parents been alive, my desire to please my parents would have outweighed all my personal desires, and I would never have left the marriage or engaged in relationships with other men.

I agreed to a divorce, satisfied that we had two weeks before we would meet again to work out the details of the divorce. He was going to give me what I wanted after all. It never occurred to me to stop and think of a future with Josh and I separated. I left our apartment and immediately found comfort in the arms of another man. My boss was pleased with the news I was sharing, and he began to speak about a future he and I could have. He had been divorced for years, so he was in a comfortable place and maybe ready to settle down again. I, on the other hand, had just begun to feel the freedom of making all my decisions alone.

My boss didn't pressure me into doing anything, but urged me to explore the possibility of a long-term relationship with him, when the time was right. My mind had already begun to fanaticize about what it would be like to know other men. Interestingly, I spent no time thinking of the value of my marriage, or reasons to try to save it. Josh had given me the perfect out.

Chapter 5 Reflections:
1 Peter 5:8 (NKJV):
"Be sober, be vigilant; because your adversary the devil walks about like a roaring lion, seeking whom he may devour."

Are you living on a slippery slope? Are you giving in to temptation? Are you spending as much time with the Lord as you do on Social Media? Check yourself and put this scripture in your heart and mind. Remember the battleground for Satan is your mind. Write down the areas of your life where you are being tempted, and ask God to help you put on the Full Armor of God to defeat your enemy!

_____

_____

_____

_____

_____

_____

Chapter 6
Is The Grass Ever Really Greener?

My life was a whirlwind of going to work, coming home to my apartment, and spending time with my boss at his house. I completely and deliberately forgot about Josh saying we would come back in two weeks to finalize our divorce. Then one Saturday morning, my boss left to do some paperwork at the office, leaving me alone until about noon.

All of a sudden, I became physically ill, almost to the point of death. I was dizzy, sweating, nauseous, and I could barely stand up. I was short of breath, and my heart actually hurt to my core. I drank a glass of water just to bring saliva to my mouth, and then, feeling helpless, sat on the edge of the bed and called my Auntie Kaye. Remember, she was the only aunt whose house I would visit and stay the night. She was my confidant. But, because I knew I was living a life outside of the will of God, I dared not call Auntie Kaye. Right now, I was too sick to hold onto my pride, but I called her anyway.

She picked up the phone, and I poured out a long confession about what had happened to me over the last several months. She listened patiently without comment until I was finished talking. I was crying, barely able to articulate what was on my mind, but determined to tell her everything.

When I finally paused, Auntie Kaye said, *"I believe I know why you feel the way you feel right now.*

I've been praying that the Lord would bring conviction on you, and turn you back to Him, away from the sin you've been living in." She was literally saying that she had been praying for me nonstop, and God was answering her prayers by bringing me to my knees literally. I wanted to reach Josh, and blurted out to Auntie Kaye that I had called several times, but was unable to get hold of him. In that moment, she said she knew where he was because he had contacted her, probably for guidance in dealing with the whole situation. So she knew all the news I thought I was bringing to her attention for the first time.

I asked if Josh was OK, but Auntie Kaye said she needed to call him first to see if he would talk to me. In my uneasy state of mind, I thought I had a lifeline just in the news that she would call Josh. Within a few minutes, she called me with the number of how I could reach Josh. He was out of state visiting a law school friend, and he agreed that Auntie Kaye could give me the number to reach him. I just wanted to hear his voice and tell him I felt terribly convicted about my life. His first words were, *"Where are you?"* I said I was at my boss' home, and he hung up the phone. I called my Aunt back and cried and cried, certain that he would not speak to me again.

Auntie Kaye reassured me that all was not lost, but it was imperative that I leave this sinful situation and get back into my rightful place with the Lord. He would show me the way to live. I heard the words, but could not receive the sentiment at all. We hung up, and moments after that, my boss walked through the door. I told him how I was feeling, and about my conversations with Josh and my aunt. It was almost like I couldn't breathe and I knew I had to get out of the house fast. I told him I had to leave and be alone to think about my life. I said I didn't know when or if I could ever come back. He was shocked, since we had a good conversation before he left, and he anticipated we would have a great rest of the weekend. But he was not a bully, and he did really want the best for me. So he said he understood, and I packed all my belongings and left for my apartment.

When I got back to my apartment, I was faced with truly being alone. I had no mother, father, sister, or husband – no family. It hit me so hard because up to this very moment, I had never been truly alone. God had always provided a safety net for me previously, and now I knew that my heartache and loneliness was the result of my selfish sin. God was withdrawing His hand from me until I could get to a place of emptiness. I never left the apartment that weekend. I cried almost every moment of the weekend, pleading with God to respond to me and let me know He was there. No voice from above came, and my anguish increased.

After a completely miserable weekend, Monday morning came and I went to work with my plastic smile, making certain that no persons knew what was really going on in my life. Image was everything! My faithful Auntie Kaye called me weekly with words of encouragement and spiritual counsel. But my loneliness was so devastating that it spoke louder than all her wise words. This terrible existence lasted for several weeks, although I went to work daily. I wasn't seeing my boss either. I wasn't seeing Josh because he was gone from me forever.

One day at work, Josh called. The morning had just begun, and he called my direct line. I asked what he wanted of me, and he said, *"If you want this marriage to work, I need you to pick up all your stuff and march into your boss' office and quit. Then come straight home to our apartment.*

I did exactly as he asked, without question. I felt in that moment that I had to make a decision to walk away from the job, which included never seeing the boss again. I was blindly trusting Josh, and there was a sense of peace in my heart for the first time in months. There was hope for restoration and reconciliation of our marriage. I knew I needed to obey Josh, but my heart was scattered all over the place. So I drove to the apartment, and knocked on the door carrying all my things. We actually embraced, and we both wept. I couldn't believe that he appeared to have a heart of forgiveness toward me. When we stopped crying, Josh said that the fact that I quit my job suddenly, as asked, meant that I was interested in working toward reconciliation.

We talked for hours, about our marriage and all we had been through. We talked ourselves to the point of being exhausted. Josh wasn't ready to receive me back as his wife, yet. He felt we should continue to see each other, but work to fall in love again. His desire was to date me as he had done before we became engaged. His hope was that we could recapture what we had before all the heartache we experienced over the past two years. We were trying to work everything out ourselves, without having a spiritual mentor or a home church. We were trying to handle things without once seeking God's wisest counsel.

Josh began planning extravagant dates to beautiful restaurants, with a spirit much like he used to court me before we were married. This time, he had the money to bring me almost anywhere. He planned picnics out in the beauty of the Colorado Mountains. He was trying, just as he said, to create an atmosphere for us to fall in love once again. Over the weeks that would follow it actually seemed like nothing had ever happened! It seemed like the love was returning as he continued to work through totally forgiving me.

Then came the day I dreaded! This was the day when we would make a decision for me to come home again and assume my position as a wife. I had had a taste of a sinful adventure, and I could not picture myself ever going back to him, and as a submissive wife living in the shadow of my successful husband. This was the wife he had known, and the wife he was asking back into his home and his heart. It never crossed his mind that I had changed and even sought the single life while staying married to Josh. He asked the question, *"Are you ready to come back home?"* Before I could respond, he interjected, *"I forgive you, and we will never discuss your infidelity again."* He gave me a look that said my affirmative response was a "given."

The answer for me was not so easy. My mind could not and would not forget about the pain and the blame I had placed on my husband. My answer seemed to take forever to leave my lips. My answer came at first from a place of calm resolve. "NO, I'm not ready and I don't think I will ever be." The unthinkable, the unexpected came out of my mouth – "NO, NO, NO!" I heard me repeat "No" three times, with each word getting louder and more determined. Josh and I knew that meant I would never return to our marriage, despite the benevolent act of my faithful husband. I could hardly believe I had spoken all that I just uttered, and from Josh's expression he absolutely could not fathom that this would be my answer. Through our tears, we both knew there would be no going back, no going forward. We were, as the Neil Diamond song says, *"...love on the rocks."*

Divorce would be the outcome. Something I thought would never happen to me was happening. My parents had a relatively long relationship as a married couple, while I would never see the five-year mark. We began the process of getting a divorce, with Josh going through the process in a fog, wishing he could do or say something to make me change my mind. But my mind was made up, since I had no presence of God to whisper cautious words into my ear while I slept. I was living and making decisions totally from the perspective of my flesh. I wasn't interested at that time in a renewed relationship with my God. In retrospect, I may have harbored negative feelings against God that were almost as severe as those I "assigned" to Josh. Hindsight really is 20/20.

I wouldn't allow my mind to entertain any thoughts that it was God's will for my whole family to be taken in an instant. So, in the absence of anyone else around me to blame for my tragedy, I put it all on Josh. Worse, having thrust blame upon Josh for moving me so far from home, I never doubted that he was guilty of causing my family's death and bringing me several states away while he pursued *his* career path after college. I was the one initiating this divorce, and as I looked around our home for the last time before leaving, I felt nothing. I wanted to take nothing with me, even though everything around me was part of my parents' memory. I didn't even try to soften my "No" to Josh, though I clearly recognized that he was crushed. How could I be so heartless? It was easy because my heart lusted after the sins of the world and I was certain to follow my heart.

Days turned into weeks and weeks into months for me as a single woman. I too bruised internally to know that I was drinking poison for breakfast daily. Part of what fueled my fleshly living was the fact that I had a large inheritance from my parents, and we all know that when you have money, you have an abundance of friends. Because my father didn't have a will, his estate went into probate and a judge had to determine how the inheritance would become mine, as sole survivor. The court released all the funds and I was in a financially stable position.

During this time I bought a beautiful, expensive condo in Boulder. Then I purchased a 280ZX, which I loved. I

76

was "living large" and may have been on a psychological path to destruction with money being the light on that path. Of course, I was too devastated myself to know how heartbroken I had made Josh, but everything in me was in the fantasy world I had left behind. I still had no counsel or grief therapy, and certainly no Godly counsel. My heart was as deceptive as was written in Jeremiah 17:9 – "The heart is deceitful above all things, and desperately wicked: who can know it?"

The devil had me in his grip, but I didn't understand it until years later. I was fast depleting my inheritance, but I didn't care. Much later in my life I learned the term "self-sabotage" and I realized in an instant this is what I was doing at this point in my life. It was all because of the pain inside that no one around me could help me shake off. I began living a life that in my worst nightmares or wildest dreams was coming true. It's interesting that people in the world think nightmares coming true are coincidences. But people in the Body of Christ know well that the remedy since the beginning of time has been repentance and obedience to God Almighty. I wasn't ready to repent or promise obedience to God!

Chapter 6 Reflections:
Colossians 3:15 (NKJV):
"And let the peace of God rule in your hearts, to which also you were called in one body; and be thankful."

Are you running from God? Are you caught in the "sin trap? Take time to sort out the answers to these questions. Write a prayer to the Lord and ask Him to reveal any heart issues you may be harboring. His arms are open, so run and receive the peace that only God Almighty can give you.

Chapter 7
Casual Comfort

I had left my life in Denver, Colorado and moved to my new condo in Boulder. I felt exhilarated, empowered, and full of a new sense of freedom – a kind of freedom I had never before known. It was remarkable that I had no regrets about the end of my marriage to the one I professed to love since high school. He was the "good guy," and yet I couldn't see him as anything except the man who caused me to lose my entire family. I could not look at him from any other lens than betrayal, with my emotions just short of hatred.

Satan was busy! I had mentioned earlier that neither my husband nor I sought to connect to another church when we moved to Denver, but we had no idea about the seriousness of that neglect. Spirits are real, and they operate when we open an invisible door to allow them to come and quite literally live in our lives. I truly needed therapy, but neither sought it nor received it. Everyone around me, and even my relatives back in Arizona didn't realize the pain I was in because I had become excellent at disguise. But Satan knew well the extent of my pain, and was happy to plant doubt, deception, revenge and misery in my heart. It was from that place that I could not look at my husband of five years with anything other than contempt. No wonder our marriage failed! God could and likely would have intervened, if only my husband and I had been seeking the Lord.

We need to be around the body of Christ. I don't care if we're new believers or seasoned. We need to be around Christ minded believers. I think we become Satan's greatest target when we think we can do something alone and on our own. We can't. We can't.

Now that I no longer had to answer to Josh or anybody, and given the fact that I had no family, relatives, or friends who understood my torment, my life took a turn completely opposite of my fine Greek upbringing, causing me to live comfortably on "the wild side." Actually, I had friends, but none understood what I was really going through because none had lived through the tragedy I experienced. I wasn't sure where to begin this new free life I thought surely I wanted, but I looked around my new surroundings and was pleased with my many purchases to furnish my new condo.

I didn't need money, but thought it prudent to get a job because I had too much time on my hands. Thinking too deeply about all I had witnessed to that point in my life was dangerous. I went back to my Dad's roots and sought employment in a women's clothing store. I had lots of experience in this field. God has a definite sense of humor because this clothing boutique was directly across the street from the university where I successfully passed the one English course I took shortly before Josh graduated from law school. However, my mind was not on pursuing a college degree. Nope!

My interview at the clothing store was impressive enough for me to be hired fulltime as the Assistant Manager, which gave me the false sense of importance. I had authority and keys to the store, and I was responsible for bank deposits and some scheduling duties. This job put me smack in the middle of college campus life, and I looked at the single college girls, thinking I, too, was young and wanted fun in my life. My co-workers at the job I had when putting Josh through law school were all single women. Once I re-connected with them, we were "off to the races!"

Our weekly Girls Night Out was always on Tuesday evenings, which was Ladies Night at the local, popular Country Dance Club in town. There was always live music and a different band each week. The movie *Urban Cowboy* was in all the theatres across the country, and we dressed in our finest cowgirl attire, glittered boots and big, wide hats on our heads. We had custom-made cowgirl shirts, and we knew we were fine! We danced the night away with any cowboy who asked us to dance. I absolutely loved the dancing, the attention, the laughter and the music. I had only experienced Greek dancing, and most of that was at church gatherings. This was the most fun I had ever had -- or so I thought.

It wasn't long before the weekly evenings at the Country Dance Club ended with one of those cowboys coming home with me. I felt no affection for these men, and I barely knew their names. Of course, I knew nothing about them before we lay together all night. Deep down, I was afraid to spend the night alone, despite the fact that I had rejected spending all the nights with my husband, who would willingly take me back after I had an affair. I craved companionship, but was not interested in dating. I never gave the next guy and the one after that my phone number. I considered none of these a date that would lead to a future.

This behavior pattern went on for four to five months, during which time I was not seriously dating anyone. I didn't realize I was so caught up in sin because of the pain that was never healed. I did call my Auntie Kaye to share the experiences I had with strange men. She was horrified that, not only were these strange men spending time in a bar with me, but also they were coming into my home. What if one of them had a violent streak and simply killed me on one of the non-dates? She brought up scenarios of caution to me, warning me of real danger at the hands of these strange men. Years later, I figured out that it was Auntie Kaye's prayers that kept me alive during this dark period in my life.

I went through my days numb. Suicide never entered my mind, which is a good thing. After five months of this behavior, I awoke and looked across my bed at the "one night stand" sleeping soundly in my bed. I was not feeling well, so I awoke the guy next to me, asking him to leave immediately. I felt cheap and dirty, but more than that, I was physically ill. This was the second time in my life where I felt this overwhelming sickness. My heart was pounding, my head was throbbing, and I felt sick to my stomach.

I had an overwhelming desire to see my old pastor, who was close to my new residence. So on the same morning that I kicked what would be my last one-night-stand out of my home, I decided to shower. As I looked at myself in the mirror before stepping into the shower, I heard, *"Who is that person in the mirror? What are you doing and why are you living like this?"* I never looked towards Heaven, but waited to see if God was going to say something to me. No audible words came. Here I was having no perception of right and all the perceptions of wrong. I had no ability to laugh or cry.

Right after my shower, I called the church, thinking no person would be there on a Saturday afternoon. Yet someone answered and was able to make an appointment for me to see my pastor the following week. I made sure to be on time. The pastor and I talked for about an hour, at which time I told him everything that had happened since the day Josh and I left the church to move to Denver. I could tell my former pastor was glad to see me pouring out my soul in confession, because he knew that the scriptures said we must do that so that we are empty vessels God can fill. Without that step, we are too full of self and our world to receive God's grace and mercy. He let me talk until I was completely void of another word to speak. Several times, he passed me fresh tissues, as I was filling them with tears faster than he could refresh my hand. At that particular moment, I had the strongest sense of despair and hope fighting inside of me like Rebecca's twins, Esau and Jacob, who wrestled together before they left her womb.

Finally, it was my time to take a long sip of water and listen. Pastor asked me to remain silent for a short time while both of us allowed the empty space to be quiet and thoughtful. Then he began to speak. He immediately began with my unhealed pain, suggesting that if only I had gotten some professional help to cope with the devastation, I would not have needed to fix the "blame" for the tragedy upon any earthly person. I would have pressed further into God trying to find the lesson He was teaching me. My pastor pointed out, *"He wanted you to bring your broken heart to Him, not to strange men who you see plainly now brought you no peace. I don't know if you were meant to stay with your husband or not, but I do know that God can heal your broken heart if you will but allow Him to."*

I always had the intelligence to internalize every point Pastor was making, but now for the first time, I was allowing my emotions to race ahead of my intellect in order to allow God to begin to fill the deep void in me with His love. I was ready to read the Word of God with new eyes because Pastor made me realize that the answers to my, and everyone's questions, are in the *Holy Bible* and not the bar. At the same time, I felt so unworthy of God's love because I perceived that my sins were greater than anyone else alive. I thanked Pastor for his wisdom, patience and guidance, promising to find my way to church more often than I had to this point.

So, while this much needed talk brought me a sense of peace, I again could not fully give myself to the Lord that I had grown so distant from. I did, however, settle down and began looking for male friendships that would be more meaningful. Dating seemed like a good transition, although I was too ignorant of the Word of God to seek only Christian men who might help me get closer to God. Dating would be as if I were going back in time to create what I had missed in high school. I had never really dated, since Josh was my first serious love and we married close to my high school graduation. I began to focus on the innocence and promise associated with dating to get to know someone better and decide if we belonged in each other's lives for a season or a lifetime. Thinking about dating in that context made me feel a bit better, and certainly a lot cleaner in my mind. Maybe this time I would get it right.

I began dating a friend of a coworker named Bob, and there was a healthy attraction between us. Like me, he loved to dance, and dance we did! He was an amazing dancer. He would say to me, *"Do you trust me?"* as he dipped me to the floor. People would actually stop and watch our dance moves. It was like floating on a cloud the way our steps were in perfect sync as we moved. I believe it was on that dance floor that I began to fall in love again. However, afraid of repeating a marriage mistake, I began to date another man at the same time. He was quite different from my new dance partner. This second man lived in a very fast-paced world. It was a world I tried to fit into, but one that introduced me to drugs. My actions had included infidelity and promiscuity, but never drugs! My former pastor's words were far from my immediate memory now, but I had yet to learn how Satan makes it a point to snatch good words from the minds of those he intends to pull away from God's Kingdom because he knows they would be a powerhouse for the Lord. It's *those* folks Satan goes after, and Satan saw ahead of me to the spiritual giant I could become if I ever stepped fully into my destiny. Hence, I experimented with drugs; however, that would be very short-lived as I truly did not like or desire to be in that world!

I had slipped back into a lifestyle out of God's order, and I found myself not only dating two men at one time, but also sleeping with them. They did not know I was balancing the two of them, but it would not be long before this lifestyle would come to a screeching halt!

I found myself tired and sick most of the time. I just could not shake the flu-like symptoms I was experiencing, and since I had no idea of the war going on between God and Satan for my soul, I could never have understood that my repeated sickness when I was in the depths of sin was coming from God to cause me to turn away from wickedness and seek His face. No, I was living in the natural world again, so I went to my doctor and he ran a battery of tests. He found nothing "wrong" with me, but he did find something! He thought he was giving me good news when he announced that I was PREGNANT!

What, did I hear him right? This sickness was morning sickness and I was six weeks pregnant! I could not believe this was happening. Why had I been so careless? What would I do now? As left his office with a million questions, the one thing that I knew was that deep down I felt a bit of joy! A new life, a new beginning, someone to love again, and someone to care for were the thoughts crashing into each other inside my head! This feeling quickly diminished when reality hit! How could I be sure who the father was? I had not been monogamous. I was sleeping with two men, either of who could be the father of my unborn child.

I spent several days contemplating how to handle this. I decided I would go on a mini-vacation to clear my head. I took two of my girlfriends with me to a beautiful resort in *Puerto Vallarta*! We planned to sit on the beach, swim in the beautiful pools, and they could help me think, really think about my future and the future of my unborn baby. So, off we went, the three *amigos*! I shared my news and actually they were both happy for and supportive of my decision to carry this baby. Now that we were in agreement about my having the child, we had the difficult decision to make about the men.

I began to look at and share with my friends what I perceived to be the heart of the two men in my life. Which man was truly a man I could spend my life with? Which one truly wanted to be with me for more than just casual dating? I knew in my heart which one that would be. It would be my wonderful dance partner. He was by far the man who had captured my heart. Now, the toughest part of everything was that I had to figure the best way to tell him, not only was I expecting a baby, but also I could not be sure he was the father! How would he react? Would he embrace me regardless, or would he run? These questions would haunt me for weeks after my return from Mexico. I had to at least feel better physically before I could face this. I'm certain today that, had I sought God first, or sought Him without the girlfriends in an exotic paradise, I would have spent less time in the agony of my mind. They say life is best understood backwards, but must be lived moving forward. So true!

Finally the day came that I could tell the great dancer, Bob, that, not only had I chosen to break up with the other man, but also I was pregnant and not sure if he was the dad! I felt sick at this situation I had put not only myself in, but I had to watch his face as he digested this news. So, with nerves like I had never had, I told him EVERYTHING! He sat back in silence! I waited for what seemed like hours for him to speak. Finally he sat up and looked me straight in the eyes. He grabbed my hands and began to say the most beautiful words I ever heard. He wanted to be with me for life and was willing to move forward with me and my baby, regardless of whether this child was his child. He told me he would love and raise my child as his own! I could hardly believe my ears. Was I dreaming? How could I deserve this love? It was completely unconditional. It was genuine and for the first time in a long time something came alive in me! I felt almost like a new baby myself, feeling free and at peace!

He asked me to marry him on the spot and I said, "Absolutely, YES." Could it be that finally my life was making sense again? Could I open my heart up to rest in the love of this man? Something deep within me knew the answer was yes. This was good and it was safe. We began to plan a simple wedding with family and close friends.

Our wedding was beautiful. We got married in that Baptist Church where I made my profession of faith to the Lord Jesus. It was during the ceremony and reception that my heart began to feel a deep need to go back to this church again. After a short honeymoon, we did return to this church. It was as if the past two years had never happened. I felt whole again. Life was good as we waited for our baby to be born. We did not have ultrasound then, so we did not know what we would have, or if this baby would look like the man who promised to raise this little one.

Finally on a very cold day in December, I went into labor. The day had arrived and off to the hospital we went. I would labor for many hours, during which time I watched the Denver Broncos play a game of football. It was a suitable distraction from contractions. The delivery was very difficult and my doctor was preparing us for a C-section. I was extremely disappointed, as I had desired a natural birth with no medication. However, this little one just did not want to appear. I was prepped for the C-section and rushed into a surgical room. I do not know what prompted my doctor to make one last attempt to deliver my baby with forceps, but it worked! My 8lb baby BOY came into our world! He was the most beautiful baby I had ever seen! He was healthy and when they handed him to us, it was obvious that this tiny miracle looked exactly like my husband, his daddy!

I do not know why God was so good to me. I was sure it would go the other way, but it was a moment I will never forget. A new life was ours for the taking and we could not wait to get our son home, just in time for Christmas! What a wonderful Christmas we would have, celebrating the birth of our son, along with the birth of our Savior, Jesus! Life was surely better than anything I could remember in a very long time.

Chapter 7 Reflections:
Acts 3:19 (NKJV):
"Repent therefore and be converted, that your sins may be blotted out, so that times of refreshing may come from the presence of the Lord."

Is your heart heavy with the pain of sin that has cost you too much? Stop here and reflect briefly on the past, but do not spend too much time in the rear view mirror! If you have held anything that separates you from God, confess it and allow healing to flow into your heart!

_____

_____

_____

Chapter 8
"Oh, Happy Day!"

At this point in my life, I was able to fulfill a promise I had made to my father. I knew he always wanted a son, but God gifted him with his two daughters. So early in life, I had promised Dad that if I ever had a son, I would name him after my father. I named my new boy "Michael" for my dad, and his middle name was "James" for my new husband, Bob's father. We were happy!

We both recognized that we needed to attach ourselves to a church, but decided we needed a fresh start in a different church from my former home church. We visited churches each Sunday, looking specifically for the kinds of nursery programs each offered. We paid attention to the music and the general feel of the people as we worshiped together. All the pastors were spiritual leaders who spoke from the *Holy Bible*. But one church in particular impressed both Bob and I very much. There was no single attribute that stuck out in our minds, although this church was relatively close to our home. But as we left after service, we said at the same time that this would be our home church.

I was blessed to be a stay-at-home mother with my new baby, so the first thing I did was to get into a ladies' weekly Bible study for the first time in my life. During this time, I began to grow in my faith. I finally understood the Word of God, and learned how to search the scriptures for meaning. I was in the right frame of mind, at last, for God to speak directly to my heart. He said, *"I am bringing you to the place in*

Genesis where I created the perfect garden for two perfect people who ended up sinning." He was telling me that His desire since the beginning of time was that there be a perfect world with no death and no sickness. In that world, there would never have been an accident that would take my entire family away from me. However, reality is that we don't live in that perfect world, but the world after Adam and Eve sinned.

For the first time, I could grasp the truth that my father, in a hurry, made a grave mistake behind the wheel that cost the lives of five innocent people. It wasn't Dad's fault either. It was an accident! When this reality hit me, I just fell to my knees and wept. My heart had become stone, and now it was melting. I fashioned myself on the "Potter's Wheel" being chiseled with a fine instrument. This was my true grieving, from which the only healing could come from Abba Father. This truly was the beginning of my faith walk, regardless of the fact that I had been saved for some years.

Before long, I was given the opportunity to become the church's worship leader and choir director. This was at a time when praise and worship became popular all over the country. New, modern songs sprang up everywhere, and I embraced the new, but clung to the old songs as well. I was animated, in my element, and very expressive in my worship leading and choir directing. Many times, the young people would say, *"Marcia, you remind us of Whoopi Goldberg in SISTER ACT!"* I smiled, but my spirited style of delivering and inspiring music never diminished.

My beautiful baby, Michael, was growing so fast, and he was the center of life for Bob and me. I was extremely overprotective, not letting many people hold, touch or change and take care of my son. Only my Auntie Kaye could take care of him as well as I could. Even my in-laws fell into the category of "not quite capable." Every single night, I had the baby in a bed next to me, and I slept with my hand on his back. At the time, I must have felt that life was too good to be true, and that happiness would disappear when I woke next. It would be several years before I would come face-to-face with the root of this fear.

My husband was a great father and provider, who could build or fix anything. During the first year of our marriage, we lived in my condo, but then decided to build a home in a neighboring town to Boulder, Colorado. This adventure was one of the best memories we had together. We found the perfect sub-division, picked out a floor plan, and then spent time every day at the construction site overseeing the building of our home. He was able to get the workers to allow him to run speaker wire throughout the house before the walls were finished, so that we had surround sound equivalent to theatre quality. This gave Bob a tremendous sense of accomplishment.

We had a big birthday party when Michael turned one year old. I bought a special outfit for him. It was slate blue corduroy slacks, a white button-down shirt and matching vest and a little bow tie. Before bringing him downstairs to see his guests, I stood him up and stooped down to his size, and said, *"You know, your granddaddy would be so proud to see his handsome little grandson turn one year old today."* As I scooped him up in my arms to go downstairs, I wiped several tears with the hand that was free from holding him. You wouldn't think that joy and grief could be interchangeable, but this is an instance where it is exactly so.

Shortly after Michael's first birthday, we moved into our brand new home. We immediately began hanging curtains and placing the brand new furniture we had purchased. Although we took none of my parents' furniture from my ex-husband's home, I took that piano to every place I lived, and now it found a home with Bob and Michael and me.

I surprised myself when I fully realized that my grief was beginning to leave me, as my faith grew stronger. I found I could be a help to others who were grieving, and I learned all the things to NEVER say to a person experiencing loss. I know the truth that God never wanted "more roses in His garden," as the reason someone's loved one had to die. It's all part of the cycle of life and death.

My husband and I were avid skiers, and as Michael approached his second birthday, we decided it was time to take him to the beautiful ski slopes in Colorado and begin to learn the art of snow skiing. We put him in ski school and left him crying, as he watched us walk out the door. We thought ski school would be the right avenue to teach our little boy how to ski, so we left him and went up the mountain to enjoy skiing together. After a few runs, we snuck up to the ski school to see how he was doing, and we were crushed when we saw him standing alone and crying. Bob said we could teach him ourselves, so we went and got him. He had never been away from our side, except for the little time he spent with Auntie Kaye. Just like his mother, Michael was not comfortable with anyone else except Auntie Kaye.

During this first trip to the mountains with Michael, we realized that he was too small to stand on skis alone. His Dad's wheels began to turn, as he devised in his head a creative apparatus to assist his small son in being able to ski. When we got home, the drawing began. He quickly had a design that looked much like a harness with two long lead ropes on each side. He pondered for days what kind of material he would need to put this together. Finally, he used heavy nylon cording, sown into a harness that would fit over Michael's jacket and hug his hips. On each hip was a clip to hold long lead lines, which ended with a metal rod that became our steering mechanism as we helped him move in the snow. Michael loved this, and he learned to ski and became an avid skier like his parents.

Chapter 8 Reflections:
Psalm 118:24 (NKJV):
"This is the day the LORD has made; We will rejoice and be glad in it."

Are you experiencing great joy at this time in your life? Take a moment to write down those things that you are thankful for.

_____

_____

_____

_____

_____

_____

Chapter 9
A Journey Of Faith

We wanted more children, so we prepared for another child. This time it wasn't as easy to get pregnant. Funny how that works! When Michael was three and a half years old, I finally got pregnant. Right around that time, I opened a daycare business, wanting to stay home. A friend also started a daycare business in her home at about the same time. I told all my daycare parents I was pregnant and assured them I would continue the business in my home. I could stay at home and parent my son, and be a friend and mentor to other children as well. Life was good. I had an easy pregnancy. February 19, 1986, I gave birth to my second son. It was an easy delivery, and Kyle Douglas was born. He was an amazing gift – life. God was again just so gracious to give us this precious child, it wasn't long that I noticed Kyle had a hard time holding up his little head. I asked my friend to hold him and tell me if, at twelve weeks, he should be holding his head up. Her son was just a little older and could hold his head up well, and so she suggested I take him to the doctor.

I went to the phone and immediately called my pediatrician. The office told me to bring him right in. Kyle and I left for the doctor's office, and we waited. My heart was racing, although I had nothing definitive to worry about. But a mother has special instincts about her children. I gently stroked my baby's head and smiled a big smile.

The doctor looked at Kyle, held him under his arms and saw his head tilted slightly to the side. He then held him down, and looked carefully at his head. As I also looked, we could see the right side of his head was a-symmetrical. The doctor said, *"Oh, my, look at this. Kyle has* **Craniosynostosis.***"* I responded with alarm, "He's got what?" The doctor went into the definition, explaining that the skull has seven suture lines that don't close until a child is eighteen years old. They stay open for the brain to grow and mature. It was clear that Kyle had at least one or two suture lines that had prematurely closed.

I barely understood what I was hearing, but with the little I did grasp, I immediately thought of the next question: "So, what do we do about it?" The doctor looked at me with compassion and said, *"Most assuredly, your son will need to have skull reconstructive surgery."* I need you to take him to *Children's Hospital* in Denver. I stopped him and asked, "Skull reconstructive surgery?" It sounded so serious that I didn't notice I stopped breathing for a moment. They needed to reconstruct my child's skull. I was in shock. Kyle was in my arms throughout this conversation, and in contrast to my nervous, frightened demeanor, he was an angel asleep in my arms.

The doctor left the room to make arrangements for what would be a series of tests, including CT Scans, ultrasounds, blood work and X-rays. My mind could barely comprehend what lay ahead. He also explained that this was a birth defect that was affecting many, many children in the State of Colorado. We since participated in a number of studies meant to determine why this particular birth defect was common in our state, but none of the results were conclusive.

The doctor passed me a number of papers, with various appointments and locations, and doctors' names. The information was voluminous. From the moment I left the doctor's office, it was like everything went into slow motion. I got to my car, put Kyle in his car seat and was driving home when this amazing fear came over me. This time I cried out and said, "God, WHY ME? WHY ME, God?" Tears were streaming down my face, and I was beside myself with anguish, pain and fear of the unknown.

I couldn't stop asking the question, and it was as if Jesus was sitting next to me. He said as clearly as possible, *"Why not you?"* His voice was so clear, so real. I was hysterical, ranting at God about losing all my family, then losing our friend and injuring others, getting a divorce, and FINALLY finding happiness. Why couldn't I keep that for more than a few years? What was so terrible about me that God should give me this additional burden? "Not my baby. He is a defenseless little person, God, and You know he's Your chosen one. How is it possible that a little baby could be faced with this serious problem?"

Unable to focus on driving any longer, I pulled to the side of the road and wept, looking at my little baby sleeping in the back seat of the car. And I heard... *"This is your Isaac moment. Will you lay him down and give him to Me?"* This was a question that I knew I could not pull the car away until I settled. I recalled the story of Isaac and Abraham. God was asking me if I would lay my baby down and give him back to God. I searched deep down in my soul to find a plausible reason for this to be happening to my son and our family.

Then I felt weak in my stomach because I clearly recalled a horrific thing I had done when I was very young. It was still too painful for me to verbalize, but God knows everything, and so He knew my darkest secret. In the next second, I looked up, this time void of all anger. I was helpless, weak and convicted. I boldly, but in a whisper, asked God, "Are you punishing me for what we both know I did when I was very young? Is this why my poor little child is suffering?" I went back in time quickly and began to hear the voices say, *"What does*

God do in this or that situation? How can you trust Him?" I was either going to say "Yes" or "No."

I knew if I said "No," I would go back to that dark place in my life. Jesus was true to His word that He didn't leave or forsake me. I didn't deserve it, but He never left. He forgave me for all my choices to that point. I dug deep down into my spirit, and I said with a trembling voice, "Yes, I will trust You, Lord no matter what happens." I cried and cried and was finally able to drive home and deliver the diagnosis to my husband and family. And that was the beginning of my surrendering my child fully to God. I didn't realize it right away, but that was also symbolic of my whole surrender to God as well. I began to walk out a new journey with the Lord, one in which I could never have imagined the outcome. My life was truly changing from the inside out.

The immediate issue was getting our lives into some state of "normal," with surgeries looming large. My family understandably took the news very hard, as did my Auntie Kaye. I always wished my parents were alive to see me now, but more importantly, I really wanted to bury my head in my mother's bosom and ask her to handle everything for me. I didn't know if I had the stamina. I felt paralyzed, physically and emotionally.

However, spiritually, I had this amazing boost of strength. Something was developing inside me that I had never before experienced. I realized there could be no giving up now. My decision to accept the consequences of giving my Kyle back to God was resolute. I would not be moved. I knew with certainty that God was with me, and whatever He did would be something I could bear. My husband and I decided to pray every single day over our son. We prayed for supernatural healing, and we believed it would happen. We even began to have prayer meetings weekly in our home, where friends and neighbors joined us and came in agreement with our prayers.

While all this was going on, we were scheduling the respective doctors' appointments. I had begun to believe in my heart that there could be nothing worse than my son's diagnosis. However, upon the first visit to Children's Hospital, I saw many children whose conditions were far worse than my son. Some had terminal illnesses, while others without limbs were being pulled around in wagons to get fresh air. God was showing me that my child had a birth defect that could be fixed. God was humbling me, so that my heart could fill with gratitude instead of judgment. Everything about my approach to the whole situation changed. I was "all in," as they say.

With all the tests that were performed, we did find some good news. Three of Kyle's suture lines on the front of his skull were completely closed, but there was no immediate danger of any pressure points that would cause brain damage. Our son's surgery would be delayed until Kyle was six months old. That gave us three months to prepare and to pray. That also allowed my Auntie Kaye and her family to get ready to come and stay with us during the surgery.

In the meantime, my daycare business went forth, as usual. Our lives as a family became normalized and we returned to a healthy routine. His surgery was planned for August, 1996, and we were ready. Michael was five years old, and Auntie Kaye took care of him while Bob and I took Kyle for his initial surgery. I prepared to stay the night before the surgery and as long after as was needed.

Because my faith in God had increased immensely during the few months, while we were waiting for surgery, I continued to believe to my core that the doctors would do a final check of Kyle's vitals the evening before surgery, and then tell me gleefully that we were witnessing a miracle. Kyle would not need surgery after all. That was my prayer and my hope and my reality. Sadly, the morning of surgery came, and the doctors took Kyle and prepared him for the operation. He had a neurosurgeon, a plastic surgeon and a maxi facial surgeon. They told us it would be about four to six hours in surgery, and the nurse showed us to the family waiting area.

I begged to go into the operating room with my son, just to be a presence. I sensed that he could feel me if I could just get physically close to him, even if he were unconscious. Of course, the surgeons refused to let me come into the operating room, but they promised to take pictures and give them to me. They kept their word. It meant so much to me to feel as if I were going through every single experience that Kyle was going through. I wanted to tell him all the details when he woke up, and I even had graphic pictures to share when he became a young man.

The wait seemed like days, and our church friends came to see us and bring us food. Auntie Kaye brought Michael so we could see him. Four hours turned into five, and five turned into six, before the surgeon emerged from the operating room with a look on his face that no parents should ever have to see. He told us that the surgery had gone well. However, Kyle had gone into a coma. Apparently, he had a reaction to the anesthesia. They could not remove any of the breathing machines, since he had developed fluid on his lungs. They were not sure if he would live through the night. He was in recovery, and we were going to be allowed to see him after an hour.

All the supporters at the hospital were looking at Bob and me, as if ready to catch us if we fell to the floor because of this devastating news. Bob was shaken, but he still had the strength as the head of the household. I, on the other hand, immediately remembered my promise to God. If He took my "Isaac" from me, He would provide a way for me to survive the loss. I totally trusted in God, so I left the group to find a pay phone to call the head of our Prayer Chain at church to engage everyone in corporate prayer for our Kyle. I mentioned needing a pay phone because back then, there were no cell phones, or Facebook or other social media by which to communicate. You either personally visited persons or called them on the phone.

I remember my pastor saying, *"Marcia, I have never said this to anyone else, but I feel you are living the Job experience. God actually chose you to endure an incredible trial, but, like the biblical Job, you will emerge victorious."* I was of the mindset that, even with the amount and severity of losses I had experienced, my life was not close to the trials Job faced and survived. I told my pastor of my promise to the Lord that I would trust Him, no matter the outcome. But at this moment, the outcome had not been determined, and I was still clinging to my faith. Little did I know during this trial what God was preparing me for next.

When we were able to see Kyle, Bob and I and Auntie Kaye went to the area where he was in ICU. None of us was prepared for what we saw. The healthy baby brought to the hospital that morning was now lying lifeless, with tubes everywhere and a big breathing machine and bandages all over his little head. His head and face were severely swollen from the surgery. The doctor told us to go home and rest, and to return the next morning. But by midnight, the doctor had, in fact, witnessed a miracle. Kyle was off the breathing machine with clear lungs. That was the miracle God gave me when I asked that the surgery be bypassed altogether. Kyle would live, although he would have a long road to recovery.

The daycare business reopened, and we brought our baby home to heal. Our lives went back to normal once again. Every day, Kyle got stronger, as he resumed the life of a seven-month old child. He had no delayed maturation and no side effects from his surgery. He was perfect in his handsome appearance and his ability to do everything a baby his age could do. We were truly blessed. I had a special peace that God had blessed my obedience, which is what He values more than sacrifice. I passed the test!

Chapter 9 Reflections:
1 John 2:3-6 (NKJV):
"Now by this we know that we know Him, if we keep His commandments. He who says, "I know Him," and does not keep His commandments, is a liar, and the truth is not in him. But whoever keeps His word, truly the love of God is perfected in him. By this we know that we are in Him. He who says he abides in Him ought himself also to walk just as He walked."

Are you asking the *"Why Me?"* question? If so, take time to listen to His voice through this scripture. He will not leave you, nor will He forsake you! As you listen, write down anything that His word speaks to your heart.

_____

_____

_____

_____

_____

_____

Chapter 10
"911" -- A Flight For Life!

In the days and months that followed Kyle's surgery, his steady recovery continued. He went from a fragile infant to a growing, healthy boy, and we gave God the glory in daily prayers. Family life was so good, and we enjoyed our boys and all of their activities. As winter approached it would be time for more skiing. By this time, and with the help of my husband's creative harness, Michael was very good on his own. However, Kyle was still too young to maneuver snow with skis, so this first winter, we had him riding in a backpack with his Daddy. He loved every minute of it and we now enjoyed this wonderful sport as a family of four.

It was not unusual for us to take our vacations during the winter months so that we could travel to the mountains for a week of Colorado winter sports. So right before Kyle's second birthday, we decided to take a week off and go to *Steamboat* and rent a condo. When we arrived it was more beautiful than we could imagine, with the fresh snow and the magnificent mountains spread out before our eyes. We skied for hours daily and enjoyed the crisp cold air by day, and in the evenings Bob and I sat cozy by the fireplace, while the boys enjoyed their time together.

On the last night of this marvelous vacation I commented that I did not believe life could get any better. The following day, we packed up to go back home and get back to work. We were rested and refreshed. I was finally living the life I had dreamed of for so long.

I loved the fact that I could be at home for my children while taking care of children for those who worked. One family in particular was very special to all of us. We had their oldest son in our home for two years before they welcomed a second son. Mom would be taking maternity leave for three months, but as soon as that ended, this new bundle of joy would be a part of our daycare. Before we had left for *Steamboat*, this family made arrangements for us to keep their three-month-old for six days while his parents went on a cruise.

Bob and I discussed this arrangement, as I was doing much more work at the church now, in addition to running the daycare and taking care of my family. I was leading the choir and leading worship. With those responsibilities, I was away from home during many evenings. However, Bob said we could handle keeping the baby for just six days, as he saw it as adding another boy to our already happy group! The arrangement seemed to work fine, and I was confident that all the boys were in the capable hands of my loving husband, Bob.

On the last evening of the time we were caring for the young baby I was at church, and one of the staff members came to inform me that I had a call in the office from my husband. I thought this odd, but was not concerned. I made my way to her office and on the other end of the phone was my husband's panicked voice! He began telling me that while the baby was sleeping he went in to check on him. What he noticed would change our lives forever! The baby was NOT breathing! I immediately asked him to hang up and call "911," which he promptly did.

In my state of mind, I asked one of the other members of the church to please drive me home. This short drive was one of the longest trips of my life. My mind raced back and forth, thinking about dozens of scenarios that could have led to this little baby having a medical emergency, but nothing I could imagine turned out to be even close to the truth.

I thought we would never arrive, but finally we came to the entrance of our subdivision. We turned the corner and much to my horror, there was a helicopter taking off in front of our house! "What? Why? How?" were the words that I heard myself speak. I went inside to find a house full of police officers. Where was my husband and where on earth were my children and the baby we had been taking care of?

As I entered the kitchen, there on the kitchen floor was my husband, grabbing his knees, head hung down, crying! I immediately went to his side and saw my best friend right there with him. He had called her right after the "911" call, and she got there at the same time the baby was being put into the helicopter. The officers were extremely kind and asked if we would like some privacy, so we retreated to our bedroom. There were all kinds of people walking around our home, but only the face of my dear friend was familiar to me.

I wanted to ask why the baby had to be air-lifted anywhere, and why strange police officers were walking all over my house, but my immediate concern was Bob. He was obviously in a state of shock. So I took his hand and led him into our bedroom. Once inside the security of our bedroom, I immediately asked about our sons. Where were they? Michael was soundly asleep; however, Kyle was downstairs with an unfamiliar lady, and still I feared that Bob needed me more than either or my sons did. I fought back tears and the urge to scream, demanding that my mind and body focus on my husband alone.

In the moment I appeared calm, but there were a million questions running through my mind. "What happened?" I asked, trying to remain calm, but listening to my own heart pounding in my chest. The answer would stick in my heart and soul for years. Bob told me that while checking on the baby, he noticed he was not breathing! He picked him up to try and wake him, but the little baby was limp and blue! He then uttered the words I wish I had never heard! *"In an attempt to wake him, I shook him – not too hard – just enough to help him breathe!"* I thought, "Of course, who wouldn't do that? He was trying to revive the baby."

A police officer knocked on our bedroom door and asked if we would like to go to Children's Hospital, the same hospital Kyle had been in for his surgery. We said yes, but first we needed to make sure we had someone to care for our boys. As we left the bedroom, we saw several people who had come from our church! It was so good to see familiar faces! One of the ladies offered to stay so we could make the trip to the hospital. We told the officer that the baby's parents were due to arrive that night. He reassured us that someone would be at the airport when they arrived, and an officer would bring them to the hospital.

We then made the trip to the hospital to be with the baby until his parents could arrive. We got to the hospital and found our way to his room. I am not sure we could have prepared ourselves for what happened next. I don't know if it was a doctor or nurse, but a medical person quietly informed us that this precious baby we had taken care of for just a few days was brain dead! *"What? Can you repeat that?"* were the words we said in unison. The baby was on life support until his parents arrived and could give direction as to what to do next.

Was this really happening? How could this have happened? What really happened? I didn't want to second-guess my husband, but gently shaking a baby to wake him should never have resulted in a child having to be taken to the hospital by helicopter, much less ending up on life support in the hospital! Before any answers could be given, the parents walked in and all of us embraced and wept! I could not even begin to feel the extreme pain these parents were feeling. They were so confused, still in shock from seeing police at the airport instead of Bob or me. I could tell they were in disbelief that there wasn't something doctors would be doing to save their son's life.

I felt extreme guilt that their child was in this serious condition, after being in our "safe" care for less than a week. I had so many questions without answers, but the immediate attention needed to be solely focused upon the baby's parents. While I stood helpless, with Bob gripping my hands tightly as he sobbed uncontrollably, my heart was breaking for the family about to lose their baby. I could not imagine myself surviving the loss of either of my sons.

Part of me respected the fact that my husband was extremely distraught, which added to the credibility of his story. But something nagged at my spirit as I felt the need as his wife to protect him from any truth that could emerge to support the fact that he had done something wrong.

The hospital staff tried delicately to inform the parents that their baby would never regain consciousness, and therefore, they had the unthinkable dilemma of keeping the baby on life support in hopes of a miracle, or ending the child's life. Everyone was crying loudly now, including me. I could hold back the tears no more!

A Catholic Priest was called in to give last rights. The parents asked if we would be the Godparents at the last rights, and of course, we agreed. This gesture probably gave Bob and me the temporary comfort that affirmed that Bob had done nothing wrong. Yet I was not convinced that we – he – was totally blameless in the imminent death of a baby. To say we were all frantic was an understatement; however, I believe you could say Bob had become quiet, still very much in shock. He had always been a very calm and collected man, so the fact that he gained control of his emotions rather quickly was not surprising to me.

I, on the other hand, was panic-stricken! My mind was filled with questions I told myself not to ask right now. We were the Godparents of a baby being returned to Heaven after being on this earth a short time. The parents thanked us, and after last rights were given to the little baby, we left the hospital after one last, long embrace among the four adults. The parents told us they would let us know of the funeral arrangements.

By the time we arrived back at home it was in the wee hours of the morning. The lady who had stayed with the boys saw the sheer exhaustion on our faces and suggested we try and get some sleep while she was there. I remember feeling like I was just going through the motions to get ready to try to sleep. What seemed odd, even at that horrible time was Bob fell fast asleep like he did not have a care in the world. As I stared down at him, I remember thinking he had not told me the whole truth. But what could he have omitted?

I could not get any sleep, thinking about the fact that a baby had died in my care. Not just a baby, but a baby that I loved! How could Bob sleep so peacefully? I pushed my doubts to the bottom of my aching stomach and forced myself to just chalk it up to the fact that he did nothing wrong and felt no deep need to hash it out all over again. The one thing I never expected was what happened next.

Our friend, who had so graciously stayed so we could rest, knocked on our bedroom door to tell us we had a phone call. Bob decided to get up to take the call. I followed him downstairs and sat very close to him to try and listen to what was being said. It was a man from our church who was a police officer, telling Bob he needed to get an attorney. Why would he need that, since he had done nothing wrong? However, this man, our friend and church family member, was adamant that we find an attorney immediately!

After Bob hung up the phone he felt the need to call and talk all of this over with his father. After that call, Bob decided he would call the attorney his father had recommended. This call would be the first of many calls to discuss what would ultimately alter our lives forever. A knock at the door caused us to jump up to see who was there. Our nerves were a jangled mess, and every ring of the phone or door caused us to jump now. Much to our horror, a lady from Social Services appeared and informed us that my day care would be shut down indefinitely!!

My heart sank as I listened to her say those words. Why was this happening, when Bob had tried to save a life, not take one? What would I tell the parents? Where would the children go? How would the children react to such sudden change? What was my recourse to closing down the day care in which I had invested much time and money to establish? Would I never get a chance to speak on my behalf and on behalf of my families who were happy with my services? I had no answers, but only a sense of loss and grief that had once again crept into my very being, and I knew firsthand what inconsolable grief felt like! The pain was unbearable!

Chapter 10 Reflections:
Romans 8:18 (NKJV):
"For I consider that the sufferings of this present time are not worthy to be compared with the glory which shall be revealed in us."

Are you or have you experienced great loss or unbearable circumstances? Reflect on this scripture. Concentrate on things from above and don't allow your mind to rob you of your eternal promises.

_____

_____

_____

_____

_____

_____

Chapter 11
"Waiting to Exhale"

When we all woke the next morning, Bob had to return to work. I had no job anymore, but I still had to take care of my boys. The funeral for this tiny baby was scheduled for a few days from now, and our attorney had advised us not to call or talk to the parents, but to attend the funeral. He also advised us not to talk to anybody, but to refer all questions to him.

Before I could consider my personal next step, I heard a commotion outside my home. When I pulled back the living room curtains, I saw a media frenzy. It looked like every television station in Denver had taken residence on our front lawn. Neighbors were all wondering what was going on, and a few of them had seen the helicopter taking the little child from our home to the hospital.

Our neighbors, normally very supportive of us, were afraid to approach my home because none wanted to get involved with the media, and it was obvious that news reporters would have chased them down for a comment. So basically, the neighborhood was paralyzed because of what had happened, and was yet to happen, relative to my family.

When the media realized we were not coming outside, different persons came and went for the next full week, but there was no time that we didn't have some press right outside our door.

We attended the very sad funeral, but were totally unaware of the reason we couldn't have spoken to the parents of the deceased 3-month-old boy. The casket was the smallest I had ever seen. We decided to sit in the rear of the church, trying not to draw attention to ourselves. People we had known for years were staring at us and glaring at us, and it felt horrible that we couldn't engage in conversation with a single person. I couldn't wait for everything to be over.

Even after the baby was buried, we were waiting for the results of the autopsy, which didn't come for several weeks. The results showed that there was a massive bleed in the baby's brain, which indicated that the baby died of *Shaken Baby Syndrome*. For about six months, the police had done an investigation, and in July 1988, Bob was formally charged with child abuse resulting in death. I could not believe this because I was so sure that what he had told me the night this happened was the truth. He said he had shaken the child a little bit in order to wake him, so I continued to believe in and support my husband.

Nevertheless, a trial date was set. They were talking about also charging me with criminal negligence for leaving the child with him. I was stunned! There had never been a reason to think my husband could not be left alone with children. He was the most calm, reasonable person you could have met, and there had been nothing in his life to warrant the police charging me with negligence. He continued to profess his innocence and I carried the innocent flag for him.

The prosecutor offered Bob a plea bargain of criminal negligence, which carried a sentence of eight years. Our attorney indicated that we should seriously consider this plea, because no matter how good or deficient evidence is, when a baby dies, there is a cry for someone to be charged with the death.

Bob may have agreed, but I was adamant that if he had done nothing wrong, there was no possible reason for him to take a deal. Surely the trial would prove his innocence! Bob continued to insist upon his innocence, and as his dutiful wife, I continued to believe him. I didn't care if we depleted all our savings, or if I had to radically alter the life we had established for our boys. The most important thing to both of us became doing whatever we had to do to vindicate Bob.

On January 18, 1989, he was convicted in less than one hour and given the minimum sentence of twenty-four years. So, at that point, we put a separate legal team together to file an appeal in the Supreme Court of the State of Colorado, which was heard in June 1990. We lost, so we prepared for him to go to prison. I couldn't even focus entirely on the knowledge that my innocent husband would be spending twenty-four years in prison, because I needed to pull in financial resources in order to take care of my boys and me.

I got licensed to work in an insurance office as an agent's assistant. I worked part-time because I wanted to be home when the kids got home from school. And for the next three years, I was busy running with the kids and my job, but always visited Bob in prison every weekend. At that time, Michael was nine years old and Kyle was six. They understood little about why we needed to drive two and a half hours each way to spend two and a half hours with their Dad. But I was a believing wife, and I thought it was important for the boys to see their father weekly.

One day, I had a revelation that the only memories my kids would really have of their father were of prison life seen from a sterile waiting area. I rejected that idea in favor of visiting prison less often. I took the boys on nature trips in between prison visits, and made sure my husband understood the reason we stopped coming to see him weekly. My family and I had only completed three years of a twenty-four year sentence!

I tried everything in my power to reach officials who had the authority to reverse his prison sentence, but nothing changed. I begged God to give me the answer as to why an innocent man should lose a quarter of a century of time for being falsely accused of a crime against a baby. Then my Auntie Kaye called to say she didn't know why she had to give me a specific scripture, but she was obedient to the Lord: Matthew 5:25-26: *"Settle matters quickly with your adversary who is taking you to court. Do it while you are still with him on the way, or he may hand you over to the judge, and the judge may hand you over to the officer, and you may be thrown into prison. I tell you the truth, you will not get out until you have paid the last penny" (NIV).*

I went to prison alone right after that, and read the scripture to Bob. I looked him straight in the eyes and asked him what he thought the scripture meant. He looked down at the floor and said, *"I did it. I got frustrated with the crying baby that night, and I shook him. I didn't mean to harm him, but I did."*

Bob broke down and sobbed as he admitted killing a little baby in our care, but something inside of me instantly hardened. My relentless efforts to free my innocent husband from a long prison sentence, my sacrifice every week as I dragged our boys to prison to maintain a relationship with their father, and my financial sacrifices to balance caring for my family with paying lawyers to fight for Bob, filled my head with so much confusion and pain that I thought I might faint.

It was when he confessed to murder, albeit an accident, that I knew I had been betrayed and lied to for the past five years. We had been married for twelve years, five of which were consumed with the baby's death, the trial and Bob's incarceration. I offered him none of the comfort he clearly sought from me. Instead, I collected my things and prepared to walk out of the prison, pushing back a flood of tears that Bob had lost the right to witness. I lost all the love I ever had for this man, and as love left my body, mind and soul, emptiness and disgust replaced it.

I needed a moment to stand up straight, as I turned my back to Bob and reached for the prison door. As I walked out of that prison, I told him I would never return. I said nothing else, and didn't look back to see or hear what Bob might have said or done in response. My heart was broken, my trust forever ruined. A year later, we were divorced. I had been living a massive lie, deliberately choosing to believe in my husband. Now for the first time in years, I could exhale!

However, along with the "exhale," there was more pain than that which came from my ex-husband's betrayal. I realized for the first time in years that I was alone, truly alone. I would be a single parent and sole caregiver to my children. The thriving daycare I had established would be a distant memory, since what Bob did was certain to prevent me from ever running a daycare again. This was not the plan I had envisioned for my family or me. This was never supposed to happen! I felt the return of that age-old question: "Why me, why now?"

I felt the same despair I had felt years ago when I lost my family in that horrible car accident, and the same sense of pain I experienced when our friend was killed in the Jeep accident in Canada. Then my mind returned to that gut-wrenching moment when my son, Kyle, was lying in a hospital bed with no sign that he would awake!

This was a whole different kind of consequence to a choice. After Bob confessed, I resented my husband. But I didn't resent the Lord. This was the result of an action of someone whom I had no control over. And in the knowing, I had more peace. I realized why he was in jail, which was a consequence of his action. There's a price to be paid for sin.

While he didn't have premeditated murder in his heart, nevertheless, his action of a split second caused whole lives to be changed forever. God gives us free will and we make choices that affect others' lives. We have to keep our eyes focused heavenward. We are not in this world. We are walking through this world. We are set apart, peculiar people, and we have to keep our focus.

It was at this moment that I gathered my thoughts, pulled up my war boots and began to walk with the determination of a soldier who moved through enemy lines chanting, "I will live and not die!" I did not run, or leap, I just put one foot in front of the other and took small steps into my "new normal" existence. I didn't know what the future held, but I was certain I would survive this. I was keenly aware that God had not allowed me to die or lose my mind because He had a purpose for my life. Oh, I left many tears on my pillow each night, but when I awakened, I dried them all up and marched on through my day, listening intently for the voice of God, who, I believed, had not put upon my shoulders more than I could bear to carry.

Chapter 11 Reflections:
Matthew 18:21-22 (NKJV):
"Then Peter came to Him and said, "Lord, how often shall m y brother sin against me, and I forgive him? Up to seven times?" Jesus said to him, "I do not say to you, up to seven times, but up to seventy times seven."

Have you felt betrayed by someone close to you? Are you harboring un-forgiveness? Ask the Lord to allow you to speak to the one against whom you are harboring un-forgiveness. If possible, YOU ask forgiveness from that person, and whether or not they forgive you is not your burden. It is only for you to ask and release all of it to God!

Chapter 12
Things Intended To Kill Us!

The kids had to know the truth about their father's confession in prison. They were seven and eleven years old. Although I kept my promise to never return to the prison, Bob called regularly to talk to his sons. I felt it was important for Bob to be the one to tell our oldest, Michael, that he had committed the crime for which he was in jail. The next time he called for the boys, I spoke first. When I told him what I needed him to do, he agreed without a challenge.

Michael and I sat on the couch, and I stayed right there while Bob told him what he had done. Michael was angry, although he appeared to contain his anger. He listened to his father without saying anything at all. Then he handed me the phone and left to go to his bedroom. I was worried about how an eleven-year-old child would process the news that everything he believed about his father was a lie.

I thanked Bob for stepping up and taking responsibility for his actions, adding that I would have the talk with Kyle. I did that within a few days of Michael finding out the truth. Kyle was a little boy, less interested in what I had to say. But Michael didn't want to talk about it, although he agreed to visit his father periodically, escorted by Bob's sister. It would take years for him to accept the truth, and eventually, he developed a good relationship with his father.

In the months that I waited for the divorce to be finalized, I kept busy working and leading worship at the church and being a mother of two active boys. This helped me get through the lonely days and the quiet nights. Then something happened that changed the direction of my life. I was asked to lead a citywide worship service in Boulder. I was excited to be able to fill my time with rehearsals and putting together a citywide worship team.

At our first practice, the room was full of instrumentalists, singers and sound techs, one of whom paid much attention to me. He began to make small talk, and finally we had a social opportunity to be together. I offered that I was getting a divorce, giving the hint that I wasn't interested in another relationship. However, he asked to mentor my sons, and I promised to think about it.

We had much in common, and I was really happy to have a man embrace my children. Sure enough, after months of dating, he asked me to marry him and I was delighted to say, "Yes." Mind you, my divorce was not finalized yet, but John was willing to wait.

I struggled personally, reconciling dating one man before I divorced another. At the same time, my church leaders had the same dilemma. They asked me to step down as the Worship Leader, which I did without a hesitation because I knew they were right. Still, my ego was bruised because I had done an excellent job.

The day came that the divorce was final, and within a month after that, we had a small wedding at a friend's home, and my new life began. The boys adjusted well, and seemed happy to have a man in the house to share in their sports and games and more.

I was "the talk of the town" for having married so soon after I got divorced, so John and I decided to move to Florida. Work opportunities opened readily for me, but not for John. He struggled to find employment, but in the midst of this, we purposely planned to have another baby. Makayla arrived looking just like an angel. Her brothers adored her, as did everyone in the family. She was the first girl to arrive in the extended family in thirty-six years! God smiled upon all of us because Makayla looked exactly like the fifteen-year-old sister I had tragically lost. She had her feisty disposition, too.

I was determined that this marriage was going to last, and it did. We spent twenty years together, during which time I worked steadily and John worked sporadically. It took a toll on both of us, and in our nineteenth year of marriage, he had an affair. He chose our daughter's horse trainer with whom to get involved, so the news reached her and me quickly. She was twenty-five years his junior. My family members were crushed! Still, I decided to make this marriage work against all odds.

After four months of trying to get over the affair, we were moving to our nineteenth home in twenty years! As sad as that fact was, I took comfort in knowing that we always provided a roof for our children. This time, however, to my utter surprise and dismay, John had taken the deposit money for the home we were about to enter, and spent it on frivolous things. I angrily confronted him, saying I was leaving, I just could not live this way any longer. There Makayla and I were standing on a street corner with no home!

I had a speaking engagement that evening, and the realtor allowed me to enter the home I would never live in, so I could get clothes for the event. My daughter and I went, and I spoke to a packed audience about my testimony, which I presented from the lens of unpacking specific pieces of luggage. Only God could have given me the supernatural strength and focus to deliver a flawless "performance." And Makayla, who was now sixteen years old, helped me by praying silently while I was speaking. When we finished the engagement, we went to my son Michael's home for the night. He was bent on finding John, but I dissuaded my son from doing anything he might regret later. Simply put, John wasn't worth it!

The next morning, I had to find permanent lodging in a less affluent area than the one in which I thought I would be living. Makayla went to her job, like normal, and I met the same realtor whom my husband had scammed. She was my friend, and had two places for my consideration. The one I chose was a duplex without central heat or air, but with more square footage than the other space. I had no time to feel anger against my husband, but I did need him to go to the house we lost and bring me my furniture and belongings. He agreed.

My job had not changed, but my household income had drastically changed. So I turned in my car to the auto dealer, who listened to my story and took the car back without insisting I pay the balance due. Then he sold me an affordable car. With every action I was taking, it was evident that God was directing my path.

I filed for divorce, and when it was finalized, I realized that, once again, the Lord had given me the inner strength to survive. I was also seeing the Lord give my daughter this same resilience. She had always exhibited great faith, but now she was walking out her faith. While we had suffered great personal loss through the divorce, we became closer than ever. She became my reason for putting one foot in front of the other and walking out this emotional trial.

The Lord remained faithful to us during the days, months and years that followed. We grew closer and closer to the Lord and to each other. Smiles turned to laughter and life became normal once again.

Chapter 12 Reflections:

Proverbs 18:10 (NKJV):
"The name of the LORD is a strong tower; the righteous run to it and are safe."

Lamentations 3:22-24 (NKJV):
"Through the LORD's mercies we are not consumed, Because His compassions fail not. They are new every morning; Great is Your faithfulness. The Lord is my portion," says my soul, "Therefore I hope in Him!"

Have you recently struggled with the consequences from another person's decision? Are you having a hard time moving on? Meditate on the first scripture and ask God to release you from fear and doubt. Remember He is walking right beside you and when you cannot see His hand, you must trust His heart! He will see you through what He has called you to. Read the second scripture. Realize our God is merciful! Every day thank Him for His mercy and His faithfulness toward you! You are a daughter of the Lord of Lord and the King of Kings!

_____

_____

_____

_____

_____

_____

Chapter 13
Facing My Unspoken Past

I must admit I never thought I would find myself at age fifty-six single, alone and parenting a sixteen-year-old who was just as devastated as I was! Neither of us minded living in our scaled-down accommodations because we realized this was better than continuing to be part of the dysfunction my ex-husband caused the whole family. So the physical and financial adjustments we made were understandable and "bearable."

While trying to keep all the "plates" spinning in the air simultaneously, I found myself actually enjoying quiet evenings and time spent with family and friends. However, "alone" was a state of mind I would have to adjust to, as honestly I am not sure I had ever been truly alone in the sense of a marital relationship. Remember, I barely graduated high school before I was married, and with short periods between my three husbands, I was always married and living my life through the filter of what my mate wanted or needed. My needs were always secondary, if my husbands or I even recognized that I had needs.

This new, quiet lifestyle gave me much time to reflect on life, particularly *my* life. The ups and the downs were worthy of self-reflection, as I knew this was the only way I could finally avoid living my life in a circle of making bad decisions and reaping the horrible consequences for them. Choices I had made and things that just happened through no choice of my own posed the same blur in my mind, but then gave me amazing clarity, moving forward!

It was during this time that I was asked to speak my truth much more than I had done before. I found it strange that the Lord would give me these opportunities, because, to me, my personal life looked terrible, and I couldn't imagine anyone wanting to listen to my testimony of overcoming obstacles!

As you, my readers, ponder everything I've shared so far about the intimacies of my life – all my life – I ask them to imagine each of my thirteen chapters being put into different pieces of luggage. Yes, luggage, as in suitcases! The Lord directed me to tell my story by opening up pieces of luggage and sharing the most personal details of my life! As I began to put all this together, I could see a life that was woven together by God Himself. He was there in every situation, shaping the direction I would take, and even letting me go in the wrong direction so He would get the glory when I found my way back to Him.

As I prepared to begin to tell the story in a new way, through the visual of different sizes and shapes of luggage, the Lord brought something special to me. In 2006, I was literally called to begin a new career path. I had been a realtor for several years and I loved it so much that I could not imagine doing anything else. Well, let me go back one year. I had been asked in 2005 to sit on a steering committee for a new crisis pregnancy center that was getting ready to open in my county. A crisis pregnancy center would meet the needs of women facing an unplanned pregnancy in our county. I enjoyed meeting with the committee and being a part of this groundbreaking project.

Little did I know that while I sat on this committee, the Lord had something very different in mind for me than allowing me to offer words to the decision-makers and then continue my life as I knew it.

In January 2006, I was asked to be the Executive Director of this new pregnancy center. I was stunned, to say the least! I was currently a successful real estate and honestly loved my job. So, to leave a career that I loved to go into "ministry" as Executive Director of this center, I just wasn't sure. As they continued to pursue me and I continued to avoid giving them a direct answer, I agreed to pray. It was not long before I knew this was a job that I MUST do.

At our next meeting they were all waiting for an answer. I knew what I was going to say would be a deal breaker, but nonetheless, I had to be honest! The words seemed to stick in my mouth. I had only told a handful of people in my life about my past mistakes, but I had never revealed the deepest secret of my heart. I didn't want to share it now, so my intention was to politely decline the position. I opened my mouth to say what I had rehearsed in my mind all the way to the center. But before I knew it I was telling a room full of strangers that in 1975, five months before my Big Fat Greek wedding, I found myself in an unplanned pregnancy. I was a naïve teenager who loved the first man who paid serious attention to me. I wanted to marry him, and I certainly wanted to abstain from sex until marriage, but things happen when passions rule any situation.

I was once the girl seeking help from a clinic or pregnancy center much like the one where I was now being offered the top position of leadership. How could I assume such a position without feeling hypocritical, and convicted before God all the way to the core of my being? I was unworthy.

My mind was racing so fast and loudly that I found myself straining to hear what the "speaker" was saying. All the guilt and shame of a teen pregnancy came rushing back to the front of my memory. The words that came out of my mouth next were words I had never spoken publically. They were words that had been spoken in secret to a very close friend.

"In 1975 I chose to ABORT my first child!" I almost could not believe it was I who was saying that word out loud. I had never told anyone about the most painful time in my life, because it ended in an abortion, which no self-respecting girl or family of the girl would allow to happen. We don't kill our babies – we have them and raise them. Even my father, whom I was fearful to tell I was pregnant before marriage, would have insisted on me having the baby and my parents raising it, if I couldn't handle the large task I had created for myself. No, I *chose* to abort my first child!

Having now revealed the whole truth, and nothing but the truth about my life, I waited for what seemed like an eternity for them to tell me I just was NOT the one for the job! No, they did not say those words. What happened in the next few moments was something that would change my life forever! They said they were certain that it was me the Lord wanted for the Executive Director's position, for I knew the pain and the anguish of finding myself in an unplanned pregnancy, and therefore I could relate to these women who would show up to receive the services we offered.

Why was God doing this to me? Surely, my assuming the role offered to me was more than I could emotionally bear, and God must have known that. He did! But He also knew that the best remedy for the pain I had lived with for decades was for me to be in this precise position at this moment in my life. I decided to plunge myself into the job and make a difference in the lives of young and older women who believed, like I did, that they had no option other than to abort their babies. God was moving on my behalf, even though it felt like He was abandoning me.

I believed the lie that God could forgive me for everything else, but never for the sin of abortion. I felt I

126

couldn't forgive myself. I have finally come to realize that we have no part in the forgiveness of ourselves. It's only because of Jesus' death on the cross. He covered that sin of abortion, just like everything else I had done in my life. He nailed it to the cross. It was I who took it back. It's flawed thinking to believe we have any part in the forgiveness process because Jesus paid it all. All to Him I owe. Sin had left a crimson stain; He washed it white as snow. There is no sin to great or too small that His blood does not cleanse.

Needless to say there were many tears cried that day! There would be many tears cried over the next several years! I accepted the position, which was actually my accepting God's assignment for my life. This was the place where God needed me to be, and so I willingly went where I was called. Through much prayer, I actually was able to accept the forgiveness I so desperately sought for myself for the abortion, and I was, in fact, the perfect choice for this position.

What was a surreal moment in time for me became the passion of my life. Before I began assuming the responsibilities of this new career in mid-July, I chose to go through a *Bible* study entitled, *"Forgiven and Set Free."* This was a study for women who had suffered the pain of a past abortion experience. This study would truly allow me to walk out healing in my life and forever set me free from the pain that had haunted me for years!

Well, I thought after completing the Bible study that my loins were girded and my purpose firm. I humbly submitted myself to Almighty God and drove to my new heavenly assignment. I put the key in the lock to open the Center on November 6th. This would be a day I could never forget, as it was my deceased sister's birthday! I marveled at how the Lord exchanged a sad day for a beautiful new day to celebrate life.

I am not sure all the training in the world could have prepared me for the next thirteen years, but I was certain that God hadn't made a mistake or overlooked a detail about my life before sending me my newest, most challenging assignment ever. I knew in the depths of my soul that I was put on the earth for *"such a time as this."* So many women would walk through the door, many wanting to parent at a young age, but many seeking an abortion.

I have seen miracle after miracle, as the Lord reaches into the hearts of women and changes them and saves a baby. However, I have also seen hearts so hard and so scared that nothing I said or did would change their minds. Many know it is wrong to abort God's child inside them, but they find no other way out of a terrible situation. I know for certain that of all the women I have seen over the years, abortion is almost always sought because birthing the child would be "an inconvenience." In my years of doing this I have not seen one girl who came because of rape or incest, nor after finding out about fetal abnormalities. Only two have come for information regarding deliveries that threatened the life of the mother. Abortion is never an easy choice, but it is a choice. I call it a God-given choice, not one imposed by our government. It's a choice given to every woman whom God has created.

I have met hundreds and hundreds of women who have told me they regret their current, or previous abortion decisions, just as I tormented myself for years regretting the same thing. I have never met a woman who regretted giving life to her baby! I thankfully, I get to offer our clients the same Bible Study that completely changed me.

My leadership role has changed over the years. In the beginning, I had to know everything about anything, and where absolute knowledge failed, I leaned more heavily upon God for wisdom to make the right decisions! Over the years, my job has evolved into the position of primary fundraiser for the organization, and God was right when He told me that my testimony would resonate with clients, colleagues and persons with a heart to donate to this worthy cause.

I also oversee the daily operations of what is now a *Women's Clinic*. I pray that I have in some way left a bit of a legacy, and I have lived in a manner worthy of His call on my life.

I would never say this position has been easy, but it has always brought me great satisfaction in knowing that in all I have done, I've given sound advice and genuinely loved all the women, young and old, who came through my establishment looking for the best solution to an unexpected pregnancy. I like to think my words, carefully chosen to be void of judgments, helped women make the "God" decision regarding the future of their unborn children! Yes, even those who left and aborted their babies sometimes returned to my clinic to talk to me. I have loved them as God has loved them and me, and He is waiting to forgive them as He has forgiven me!

One day, I was driving and contemplating the number of persons who knew me and were encouraging me to add to my next speaking engagement the full truth, which included my teen abortion. I prayed and asked God to show me what it would look like in order to make sense to my audience.

Still driving, I had a vision of a set of luggage on a table, and I could definitively identify attributes of my life inside each piece of luggage. This luggage was not the beautiful, color-coordinated set of luggage you might find in a high-end retail establishment. Each piece was unique in that some pieces were torn, some had broken handles, some had worn corners, and one had a "transfer" tag still on it.

I was looking at luggage that resembled my life – tattered, torn, broken, and ready for transfer. But as soon as I saw that image of my life, I saw a large, bright red cloth before me, and me taking that cloth and covering every piece of luggage except the piece in which my abortion story would appear. I realized that the red cloth symbolized the blood of Jesus. But also in that moment, the Lord appeared to me and urged me to push that piece of luggage under the red cloth with the others. I knew in an instant that God had sealed my complete redemption. It was a beautiful spiritual marker for me.

I didn't pull my car over to cry hysterically like I had done all those years before. Instead, a calm fell over me as I continued to drive. God was letting me know that once I revealed my complete truth, I had the credibility to draw the pain from other hurting women because of my level of empathy. It brought me straight to the biblical story of the woman with the issue of blood, who had used all her resources to be healed from a terrible malady, and whose only hope was to touch the hem of Jesus' garment as he passed her way. Jesus was her only hope for healing.

I had been sought after by many churches and civic organizations to come and share my story of how I became the Executive Director of a Crisis Pregnancy Center. What appeared to them as seeking out a public speaker to impart knowledge in the natural world was really God putting me in multiple positions where I would share my entire life's story. It was as I shared my story that He would offer supernatural healing to women who came to hear me.

From that day to the present, my format for speaking follows the literal opening of different pieces of luggage containing the events described in this book. I always end by putting the red cloth over every piece except the abortion bag. It is the first piece of luggage on my table, but the last to be opened, since this was my deepest, darkest secret. After I've told my truth, I push this bag under the red cloth with all the rest of the luggage.

At this point, I always have the full attention of every person in the audience. I immediately read this passage aloud:

"Now a woman, having a flow of blood for twelve years, who had spent all her livelihood on physicians and could not be healed by any, 44 came from behind and touched the border of His garment. And immediately her flow of blood stopped. 45 And Jesus said, "Who touched Me?"

When all denied it, Peter and those with him said, "Master, the multitudes throng and press You and You say, 'Who touched Me?' "

46 But Jesus said, "Somebody touched Me, for I perceived power going out from Me." 47 Now when the woman saw that she was not hidden, she came trembling; and falling down before Him, she declared to Him in the presence of all the people the reason she had touched Him and how she was healed immediately" (Luke 8:43-47 NKJV).

When I have finished reading, I ask women who received a piece of paper when they entered the auditorium to write down those things they may be hanging onto, which have to date been hidden. They have carried this "luggage" for far too long and need to lay it at the feet of Jesus, just as I finally did.

I stop talking and glance around the room as nearly every woman writes down her most private secret. It is at this time that I refer back to the portion of scripture that says this woman with the issue of blood was not hidden when she sought healing from Jesus. She was in a crowd of people, desperate for a cure, and cared not who saw her or talked about her.

I direct each woman who has written on a paper to bring it forward and place it in a basket I have on the stage, to mirror the woman with the issue of blood who was unafraid to be hidden any longer. As the audience continues to come forward and return to their seats, I make it clear that I have no power to heal or forgive, but all power comes from Jesus Christ and the work that he did on Calvary's cross when His blood flowed freely for all sinners. His blood is my red cloth that covers all my mismatched, broken and damaged luggage.

Before I leave each speaking engagement, my host closes the event in prayer, after which I stand ready to pray and encourage each woman who has taken the brave step to be vulnerable before a crowd of strangers. I leave with the basket of confessions, and as I return to my office, I read them all. They don't have names on them, but they represent vivid pictures of hurting women. They may think that what's on that paper is unforgivable. They wrote it down, gave it up, and then left. My job now is to pray over each confession, asking the Lord to make Himself real to each woman. They have, in fact, touched the Hem of Jesus' garment, and my prayer is that He will reveal Himself to them in a way that ensures they know that they have been forgiven, healed, and set free. Reading those papers after each time I speak, is also confirmation that I, too, have touched the Hem of Jesus' garment and been healed. I will never take for granted the healing and freedom I, myself, have received. Because the fact is, no matter what, I have touched the Hem of His garment and been healed!

THE END

References

"Here's lookin' at you, kid!" Movie *Casablanca, 1942.*

"Oh, Happy Day!" Original song by Edwin Hawkins & the Northern California State Youth Choir, 1968.

Sister Act. Movie, 1992.

Waiting to Exhale! Movie, 1995.

Epilogue

It took me years to write my story, not because I lacked sufficient time to devote to writing. No, my dilemma was whether or not I had the courage to reveal my inner secrets to strangers. I fashioned myself standing naked before people, and the thought of them staring at all my imperfections, inside and outside, made me run from writing a book about my life.

But for those readers who know the power of God, when He charges us to do something, we have no choice. I foolishly thought that if I "ran out the clock" on following God's direction, He would choose another to write the story. However, God made it crystal clear to me, in visions and dreams, that no one could tell my story better than I, nor instead of me. It was mine to write, and there was a waiting audience of persons who were as desperate to hear my story as was the woman with the issue of blood desperate to touch the hem of Jesus' garment.

Once I resigned myself to obey God, the writing flowed. I must challenge readers to engage in introspection to open up your "luggage," as I have done. So I ask you, "What's in your luggage? What is it that you think is unforgivable in your life? Do you believe God has the power and the will to heal you of all the pain you've carried for too long?

If you are ready to lay your burdens at the foot of the cross with Jesus, then take the space below and write your confession. God will see it, and when He hears the cry of your heart, He will meet you. He will forgive you. He will heal you. And He will set you free. I would love to hear your story of how Jesus met you in the pages of my book. Please feel free to contact me.

John 8:36 (NKJV): "Therefore if the Son makes you free, you shall be free indeed."

_____

_____

_____

_____

_____

_____

_____

_____

_____

_____

_____

_____

_____

_____

_____

_____

_____

_____

_____

No Matter What

A lot of us grew up believing

At any moment we could lose it all

And at the drop of a hat

God might turn His back and move on

A lot of us feel like we blew it

Thinking that we're just too far gone

But I want you to know

There's still a hope for you now

No matter what you've done

You can't erase His love

Nothing can change it

You're not separated

No matter what

There's never been a better time to get honest

There's never been a better time to get clean

So come as you are

Run to the cross and be free

Oh, be free

No matter what you've done

You can't erase His love

Nothing can change it

You're not separated

No matter where you run

He's always holding on

You're still a daughter, you're still a son

No matter what

I don't know what you've been taught

Don't know what you've been told

All I know is my God

Will never let go of you, no

And I don't know what you've seen

Don't know what you've been through

All I know is my God

Will never let go of you

He'll never let go!

He'll never, never, never let you go

No matter what you've done

You can't erase His love

Nothing can change it

You're not separated

No matter where you run

He's always holding on

You're still a daughter, you're still a son

No matter what

You're still a daughter, you're still a son!

No matter what

Written by: Ryan Stevenson, Bryan Fowler, Jonathan Smith

Lyrics © Sony/ATV Music Publishing LLC, ESSENTIAL MUSIC PUBLISHING

Lyrics Licensed & Provided by LyricFind.

How to Reach the Author

Marcia Buterakos Marron has poured out her heart in this very personal narrative about her life. Readers will find themselves in parts of the book, but especially women who have felt deep grief over having made the decision to abort a child will find healing here.

Marcia is an excellent keynote speaker, having served in dozens of venues in several states across the country. Her message, entitled, *"What's In Your Luggage,"* draws women to the hem of Jesus' garment.

She can be reached at the following email address:

destinationfreedomnow@gmail.com.

53056644R00078

Made in the USA
Columbia, SC
10 March 2019